D0803020

STRAIGHT TALK

TALK

from GOD

*Daily Guidance to Encourage, Empower and
Transform Your Spiritual Journey*

BONNIE HASSAN, MSW

Straight Talk from God: Daily Guidance to Encourage, Empower
and Transform your Spiritual Journey

© 2019
By Bonnie Hassan, MSW

All rights reserved. Reproduction or translation of any part of this book
through any means without permission of the copyright owner is unlaw-
ful, except for promotional use. Request for other permissions or further
information should be addressed in writing to the author.

ISBN-13: 978-1-7340772-4-7

Cover Design: Ryan Biore Lause, ryanlause91@gmail.com
Layout: Anna Magruder, annamagruder@hotmail.com

Bonnie Hassan, MSW
Hermitage, TN
bonnie@bonniehassan.com

www.bonniehassan.com

To my son, Jason, an amazing dad,
who continually inspires me to dig deeper.

To my beautiful granddaughter, Hayden,
who always challenges me to reach higher.

To my mother, Josephine,
who loved me enough to stay the course
so we both could heal.

Acknowledgements

Walking a spiritual path has taught me that there are no insignificant people on the journey. Each one of you has served his or her unique purpose in my life, whether either of us was aware of that purpose or not. Given that, there is no way I can possibly thank each of you by name.

I offer, instead, my overwhelming gratitude to *all of you* who've agreed to co-create with me this time around. Without even one of you, my journey would have been different and lacking in some way.

I appreciate each and every one of you who have supported me, taught me, challenged me, and empowered me; those who have laughed with me, cried with me, and held me when words couldn't be found and emotions ran wild.

I value those who've left to honor their own paths, and those who've stayed the course. Each of you has contributed in your own special way to my ability to bring the wisdom and guidance contained in these pages together, and I am forever grateful.

I am most grateful, though, for that Divine Presence in my life that never gave up on me, even when I turned my back, when I resisted, when I denied—the Presence that found a way to reach me through my anger and pain, healing me more deeply and giving me hope, purpose and the desire to go on.

When I asked, "Why *me*? How can *I* be worthy?" the Divine answered simply, "To be worthy, all you have to do is be willing."

I was. I am. I continue to be.

In gratitude always, with love,
Bonnie

Introduction

I took my first Reiki class (a Japanese technique for stress reduction, relaxation and healing) in February 2000 from Sr. Mary Jo Mattes at Tabor House of Prayer in Millvale, Pennsylvania. During the class, Sr. Mary Jo stated:

"The more you take Reiki on as a part of who you are, the more God leads you down your own unique path."

At the time, I had no idea what she meant by that. Now, 19 years later, I can look back and see exactly how that statement has played out in my life.

Back then, I was a therapist working in a lockdown facility for teenage girls in Bridgeville, south of Pittsburgh. My toolkit from my master's degree in social work didn't seem to be of much help as I worked with these deeply troubled girls in the foster care system. It was my first job as a therapist, and I felt overwhelmed and underprepared.

Searching for something else to help me help these kids, I thought of Reiki. I had heard about it several years earlier, but all I knew was that it was supposed to help with stress reduction and relaxation. I asked my boss if I could learn Reiki and use it with the girls. To my surprise, she agreed. After all, if nothing else, those girls could stand to be a little more relaxed!

As I began incorporating Reiki into my therapy sessions with the girls, I saw incredible changes taking place. Over time, depression, anxiety and panic attacks began to diminish. Girls who'd had nightmares were able to sleep through the night for the first time in years; and those who had been reluctant to come to therapy were knocking on my door and asking to talk!

During my Reiki I class, Sr. Mary Jo had also explained that as Reiki practitioners we are only a channel for the healing energy that comes from God, and that as the energy flows *through us* to others, we are also receiving its benefits. As I used Reiki to help the girls, and practiced it on myself, I noticed personal changes that could only have come from this energy work. Having grown up with an alcoholic father and a mother who had never unpacked her own emotional baggage, I carried my own scars and wounds. I had problems with self-esteem and anger issues; I carried a deep rage within me toward my mother. Although I'd been in therapy for years and had made considerable progress, those issues still caused me difficulty at times.

As I continued to practice and receive Reiki, my own healing progressed. During the Advanced Reiki Training class, the third level in the Usui/Tibetan system, the rage I had carried in my belly for years was taken from me as Sr. Mary Jo used me to demonstrate aura clearing, a technique to remove stubborn energy blockages. My self-esteem and self-confidence also began to improve. As they did, my spiritual and intuitive gifts started to surface.

The changes didn't happen all at once. It was a slow progression over many months, beginning with my Reiki sessions becoming more intuitive than traditional. Instead of working on a client using the structured hand positions I had been taught in class, my hands and body would move around each client spontaneously in ways that I didn't understand and wasn't intending but seemed to further empower the intensity of the work.

As I continued to allow my individual sessions to be intuitively guided, I became aware of other energies in the room. Family members and friends of the client would come in energetically to help the person on the table or to seek healing for themselves. I began to receive intuitive messages from those who were spiritually present; these were later confirmed by the clients who were physically present for the sessions.

In May 2003, as I was practicing Reiki on myself during my spiritual practice, I had a vision of Mary, the Blessed Mother, standing in front of me.

"I have work for you to do and you can't do it here," she announced, referring to the facility where I was working as a full-time therapist.

Three days later, I gave my notice and began looking for office space to open a healing practice. I opened my office in October 2003 in Pittsburgh's West End. That move seemed to be the key that further unlocked my spiritual gifts. I began working with groups for healing rather than just individuals, as most Reiki practitioners do. As I continued to allow Spirit to guide my work, I began to chant and tone in my Reiki sessions in what most often sounded like Native American; but it wasn't unusual for participants to hear me speaking a variety of languages simultaneously, such as Aramaic, Hebrew, Latin, Cherokee, Seminole, Inuit, Spanish, Chinese and more.

After taking a Reiki drumming class in 2005—which I disliked and never used in my practice because it required me to use the drum in a very structured way—I was spontaneously guided to pick up the drum during an individual session and drum over and around my client. Her response was profound. She had a deep emotional release expressed through tears, pain-filled facial expressions and body movements that included muscle spasms and twitching.

After that, the drum (and eventually rattles) became integral parts of my healing sessions, their use always guided by Spirit. My comfort level with these changes increased and my relationship with the Divine deepened, but nothing that had occurred up to this point prepared me for the remarkable events that were ahead of me.

On September 9, 2006, I was teaching a Reiki II class. I had just finished giving my students their attunements, the process that gives them the ability to move to the second level of Reiki. I sat alone in my back office, giving them time to process and journal about the experiences they'd just had.

As I waited, I heard a voice in my head, a voice I now call my "God Voice" say, *Pick up a pen.* I did so and let it hover over the yellow legal pad sitting on the desk in front of me. Almost instantly, the pen began to move across the paper:

You are all powerful and courageous soldiers on a journey for which you came totally unprepared—at least, in your knowing of preparedness. As you peel back the layers of who you are to find who you are all becoming, we will give you the tools—and yes, sometimes the weapons—that you need to stay the path.

Do not hesitate to call on us when you become weary or fearful or even angry, even if your anger is at us, because we seem to ask more of you than you could possibly give. We will never request more than you can handle, although it may seem that way to you. And we will always give you what you need to go to battle, to wage the war. But your weapons are not weapons of assault. They are the weapons of love.

You must look deep within your hearts. Allow your hearts to open wider than ever. Give more than you have ever given, in all ways: physically, mentally, emotionally, spiritually, materially. Even when you believe there is nothing more to give, look more deeply into your hearts and give what you find there.

Do not be stingy with your giving. Do not be miserly. Give as if the source is unending and overflowing—for it is. And as you continue to give, you will see that it is so.

But remember as you give to others you must also give to yourself. You are as deserving, if not more so, as all of those to whom you give. And as the giver gives, he also receives—multiplied many times over in many different ways and many different forms. As you go forward you will see that it is so. Trust in this and act accordingly.

Give out the love you wish to receive, and it will come back to you, time and time and time again. Give and be open to receive.

This wasn't the first time I'd been told by Spirit to pick up a pen and write down a message. I'd had several similar experiences over the prior few months, usually when I was sitting alone in the silence during my spiritual practice. God seemed to feel the need to make the communication between us more concrete, rather than my simply *hearing* the God Voice. But this was the first time I'd been guided to write down a message for *others*. This message turned out to be the first of almost 600 messages that would come through me for others over the course of the next 13 years and are still continuing today.

After that first message, each time I did a group healing session or taught a Reiki class, I would be guided to sit in my office and pick up my pen while my clients and students were processing their experiences. Eventually I began *verbalizing* the messages *during* the healing sessions and Reiki classes. I would feel a sensation in my throat as if there was something waiting to be released and when I opened my mouth, the words would tumble out.

I'd remember bits and pieces of them for a short while after they came, but then they'd be forgotten. I began wearing a voice recorder to record the messages and would email the mp3 files to those who were present at the time they came through.

One day, Deb Gibson, a friend of mine who calls herself a "'Bonnie junkie", mentioned that she'd transcribed the recordings for herself, saying they had so much good information in them that she wanted to be able to read them, not just listen to them. She offered me the transcripts from the sessions she had attended and then asked if I'd like to have *all* the sessions transcribed, not just the ones she attended. Hesitant at first, I eventually said yes. She's been transcribing them ever since!

The messages in this book are excerpts from more than 1,800 pages of transcripts. The longest single message is about 5,000 words.

As the pile of typed pages continued to accumulate in my office, I kept hearing my God Voice tell me that they needed to be shared in a bigger way. I put a selection of them on my website and began posting some of them on Facebook from time to time.

In January 2018, while preparing for hip replacement surgery, the intake worker at the hospital asked me if I had an advanced directive, medical power of attorney and a last will and testament. I had the first two but not a will. Her question made me realize that it was probably time to prepare one.

Several days later, while sitting in my office contemplating that will, my glance fell onto that stack of transcribed messages sitting in the corner. Thinking that those messages would most likely end up in the recycle pile when my time on earth is done and my son is cleaning out my condo, my God Voice spoke up:

It's time for a book!

I cringed at the thought! For many years I'd felt God calling me to write a book. Three years prior, in 2015, I received such strong and direct guidance that I entered a writing contest and submitted a book proposal; but once the proposal was submitted, I couldn't write another word! I couldn't even look at my computer without feeling guilty about my lack of desire and inability to write. I eventually realized it wasn't the right time regardless of what my God Voice said.

As I healed from surgery and additional messages continued to stream through during client healing sessions and classes over the next 10 months, I knew those messages had to be shared in a more permanent form before I left the planet.

At the end of that year, in December 2018, I hosted an overnight gong meditation in my condo for a small group of friends. In preparation for the experience, Judy Bernard, the gong master, asked the four of us who were participating to set an intention for ourselves and to place those intentions on an altar she had created just for that purpose. I placed my intention in the form of a three-ring binder with a printed picture on the front that had the title *Messages from God* on it, and my name at the bottom as the author. I even printed additional copies of some of the messages and put them inside. I was finally ready to make that book a reality!

On January 1, 2019, I began going through the transcribed pages searching for short excerpts that could stand alone from the longer messages. Since setting the intention to birth the book, the guidance I received about its format was that it should contain 365 messages, one for each day of the year. As I culled through the pages, I highlighted and numbered those that called out to be included and ended up with a total of 510.

So how was I to choose which of those 510 should be in the book? Over lunch one day with Judy, my friend who played the gongs for that overnight gong meditation, I explained my quandary.

"You let Spirit guide everything else," she reflected back to me. "Why not let Spirit decide what goes in the book?"

Of course, that was the answer! Sometimes God's guidance comes through earth angels!

I went home and numbered 510 squares of paper and placed them all in a large bowl. I sat in my living room with that bowl on my lap and began doing Reiki over it and all those pieces of paper within it, all the while asking Spirit for the perfect messages to include in the book. When I felt the Reiki energy come to a halt, I began drawing out 365 numbers from the bowl. I listed them in a notebook in the order they were drawn. What you're reading is the culmination of that process.

A couple of things to keep in mind as you read these Divine inspirations: You'll notice that God is referenced by a variety of names: God, Source, Creator, Spirit, The Universe, The Divine Source of All That Is and more. In doing so, God intends that the messages will call to whomever reads them, not just those who reference the Creator by the name of God.

As Spirit says in one of the messages, "You can call me any name that calls to you, and as long as you are calling Me, as long as your intention is to connect with that Divine Source that is within you, I will come regardless of the name you speak. I care not about names. I care about *you*!"

The Divine also frequently refers to our spiritual assistants (the guides, angels, teachers and loved ones that assist us all as we travel our spiritual paths) in the messages, and may go from speaking in first person (I, Me) to addressing you from the group perspective (we or us). Just know that you have a host of spiritual beings working with you and around you who all have your best interests at heart.

Although God determined the messages contained in the book, it's up to you how you use them. You can read one each day in the order they were chosen. You can open the book at random and let God decide what you most need to know in that moment. Or, you can consult the index, "Straight Talk for Specific Needs," if you're in need of guidance for a specific issue. It's your choice.

Use them to inspire your meditation practice. Use them when your heart is calling out for assistance. Use them when you're feeling separate and alone and need a reminder that God always has your back.

However you're guided to use them, I hope these gentle, loving messages, this *Straight Talk from God*, will encourage your own deeper, intimate relationship with the Divine. My desire is that they will transform your spiritual journey in a way that empowers you to own *your* power and be a greater force for good in the world because, ultimately, that's the reason God wanted these messages to be shared with a greater audience in the first place.

With love, blessings and gratitude as you continue your journey,
Bonnie

DAY 1: *What's My Plan for You?*

Divine plans. Human plans. One and the same. You ask My plan for you, and I say to you, "My plan for you is *your* plan for you. I want what you want."

How badly do you want what you want? And is what you want coming from a place of love for yourself? Or does it come from a place of fear or anger or resentment or woundedness? Think about where your plan for you comes from. Does it come from jealousy or greed? From wanting something because there is a space within you that needs to be filled, and you are trying to fill it with *things* rather than with self-love and self-acceptance?

What *is* your plan for you? And does your plan for you include the Divine? I'm asking you. *I am asking you.* What is *your* plan for you?

DAY 2: **Risk Equals Change**

I am here for you every step of the way, but I cannot do for you that which you will not do for yourself. So, I'm asking you to take a good look at your life, at your way of being. Take a look at the ins and outs, the ups and downs. What needs to change? How would you like it to be different? And what can you do, what can *you* do, to make it different?

We here in spirit assist with all that we can, in every single way that we can, but we can't change your behaviors. We can't change the choices you make. *You* have to look at the opportunities that come up for you to do things differently, then make a different choice. And yes, it means taking a risk—some risks bigger than others—but you'll have to take the risk if you want to see the changes take place. There is no other way for change to happen.

You hold onto what you know, even if it makes you uncomfortable, because it is familiar to you. But the time for holding on has passed. It is time for you to let go, to rise above your current circumstances, to raise the bar higher for yourself so you can move to the next level.

How long will you wait before you make changes? How many more times will you tell yourself "Yes!" then fall back into old patterns? You need to stand strong. You need to decide this time that you will do it differently, that you will follow through, that you will be consistent in choosing the higher choice, even though it requires more courage, more faith, more trust.

DAY 3: Be the Most Open Channel

Be aware. Be aware of the power of your energy, the strength of your light, the strength of My power working *within* you, *around* you and *through* you, as you and I *together* reach out to the masses, as we work to raise the vibration of those whose vibration is so low, so dense, they are fearful they cannot go on. They have been brought into your aura, your energy field, because you have something they need, something they can relate to, something that *resonates* within them. So simply by being the *best* you can be—that's all you have to do, be the *best* you can be—you will assist them in some way.

Do not insist on knowing what part you will play or how you are assisting. Do not ask why they have been brought into your life, or why you have been brought into theirs. That is your *ego* wanting to know. Trust you are doing My work, the work you decided you *wanted to do* when you incarnated into this lifetime. Part of that is *detaching* from knowing, trusting you are the right channel, the right messenger, the *perfect instrument* for what needs to be done for each and every person that comes to you.

Surrender to the process. Get your ego out of the way and allow yourself to be the biggest, the best, the brightest, the most open channel for My work that it is possible for you to be. That is what I ask of you today. That is what I *hope* for you today.

DAY 4: Who Are You?

Who are you? Who are you *really?* At the very core of your being, who are you?

You are Divine. You are Divinity itself. Underneath all the life experiences, the emotional struggles and turmoil, the pain—physical, mental, emotional, spiritual—under it all, you are simply the great I Am Presence.

DAY 5: Put Action into Your Intention

Begin to be aware of your thoughts and words and the tone of your voice. All of this has power. To be your most powerful self, think positive. Speak positively. Eliminate the negative, the nots, the don'ts, and be present in the moment.

When you set an intention, it should be set as if it is already in existence. You don't want to say, "I will" or "I want." Wills and wants are somewhere in the future. You don't want to say, "I'm open to change." I'm open to change doesn't mean you're changing. There's no action there. When you set an intention, put some action into the intention. Let the words speak in the most powerful way possible to help you move forward.

DAY 6: Become More

It's not easy being different. It's not easy to pull away from those you love, those who know you, to grow and expand and become more. It's not easy to honor your heart when your gut is full of fear, not easy to honor your heart when your mind is full of doubt and worry. But you've done it before. You can do it again.

As you are growing and expanding, there are bigger steps, bigger risks to take. You are putting a greater distance between your old ways and your new ways, your old friends and your new ones. Sometimes the most difficult thing is that, as you are leaving the old friends behind, there are no new friends yet to take their places because your new vibration has not yet stabilized enough to draw those to you that you need.

In times of transition, there is more falling away than coming closer. Sometimes people are lost permanently simply because they move out of your aura, out of your orbit. Others pass and make their transition. Their work in this lifetime is finished, even though you were not aware they were even close to making a transition.

When they pull away, they pull away for their own good, as well as yours. Even though you mourn their leaving, they are making a bigger space in your life for you to become more.

DAY 7: *Invite Us In*

The journey is so much easier when you allow, accept, embrace and use the assistance that is available to you. It's so difficult for Me to sit next to you while you're sitting on the fence, wanting to nudge you off, wanting to get you going, and having to sit there and wait.

What is even more difficult is when you step off the fence and begin to move forward and *forget to ask us for help!* Because then we watch you struggle in ways you wouldn't have to struggle if you'd simply *invited us in.*

We are not allowed to assist unless you ask. For then, we would be interfering. But when you invite us in, you have made an invitation. You have made a space for us to assist. Then we can do all manner of miracles because you have asked and given us permission.

DAY 8: Be Patient

Be patient. Don't give up. Your time is coming; but Divine timing is in play and there are so many pieces that have to be put into place. So be patient and know I am working for you and with you, and that which you desire—that which your heart is calling you to—is coming. It's coming.

Trust and know that I am taking care of you. Be patient and keep loving yourself. Keep knowing how beautiful, how special, how unique you are, and how much you have to give. My time and your time are different. So be patient. I cannot rush what I am doing. I would not want to rush it and have it be less than the perfection you deserve and are entitled to.

DAY 9: Ask for Help

Do not be afraid to ask. You have not failed just because you ask for assistance. There is nothing lacking in you because you need help. Perhaps part of what you came here to learn is how to accept and receive help. Perhaps you need to learn that there is nothing wrong with asking for help.

Things happen time and time and time again to give you an opportunity to learn to ask for help because you so rarely do. You decided that you had to do it all alone because you didn't trust anyone to help. Perhaps they've pulled the rug out from under you so many times, you've just given up hope. You think I am like *them* and *I* will pull the rug out from under you, too! But I am not them, not that part of them that did that to you. I am the best part of them, perhaps the part they have not yet learned to access. And I? I will *never, ever, ever* pull the rug out from under you. I will always, *always and forever,* be there for you.

Remember, I may not answer your prayers in the way you want. Sometimes it seems I answer them not at all. It is only years and years later that you can look back and understand that if I had given you what you wanted, your life would be completely different today and not the life you wanted at all.

So understand, every prayer is answered, even ones that seem unanswered. I have *never*, nor will I *ever*, abandon you, let you down, or let you walk the road alone if you have asked for My help. You are My child, and I will *never* let My children travel alone.

DAY 10: *Release the Old*

How many times have you said, "Yes, I trust" then acted as if you do not? How many times have you said, "Yes, I believe" then acted as if you do not? How many times have you said, "I forgive" then took back the forgiveness?

That push and pull, it comes from your fear. Perhaps it comes from old messages you have received: you are not good enough to be healed, there is no one you can trust, no one has your back, you must do it all. It is your choice to hold onto those old messages, those old beliefs, or to let them go. If you keep holding tightly to your old ways of being, those old ways that no longer serve the person you have become and the person you are working to become, I cannot pry them from your tightly clenched fingers. I have to honor the choice you are making to hold tight to them.

I'm asking you if that's serving you now. *Is that serving you now?*

DAY 11: Revisit the Past to Move Forward

Bit by bit, you move forward. Sometimes it seems like you move backward instead of forward. I encourage you to remember that as you move forward, you must revisit those things in the past that you've healed at the level you were previously, because now they must be healed at the level where you currently are.

You are not going backward, per se; you are simply *looking back* from a bigger and greater perspective—a greater Divine perspective—because at this point in your journey you are capable of seeing other lessons you've learned from the experiences you've had; lessons that were not visible to you in the past. So it is not a going backward. It is a *looking back*, a reassessing, a reevaluating, so you can move forward in a bigger and better way.

Remember this when things get crazy, chaotic; when it seems like, yes, indeed, you are back at the very beginning. Before you know it, your ego will make you think you are going backward because as you take another step forward, your ego is afraid. *Change! More change is coming!* the ego says. *I do not want change! I like it where I am! No, no, let's not go there! Let's convince them they have faltered!* Remember, you have not faltered. You are simply revisiting to reassess, reevaluate and move on.

For each of you, the journey will be different. It has to be, for you are each different. As each of you uniquely vibrates higher and higher, the purpose of that higher vibration will eventually be shown to you; but you must be patient. You must allow all the parts of your growing to come together with all the parts of the universe that are working in tandem to help you go where it is you are going. It takes a while for all those pieces and parts to come together at the same time and in the same place. So be patient.

DAY 12: Transformation Comes Through Surrender

What do you need to let go of? What have you been holding onto for so long that it has become a part of you, familiar, yet uncomfortable because it no longer serves you? What is it you need to surrender because you, yourself, do not have the capability to heal it? What is it you need to release to Me, surrender to that Higher Power? Old hurts, old wounds? Fear about the steps you are taking as you move forward? Old relationships that hurt, that you need to let go of so that there is a space for new?

Perhaps you think there is nothing you are holding onto. I encourage you to look more deeply because as you go higher, as you come closer to Me, you must search more deeply within yourself for the old wounds, the old pains: rejection, humiliation, degradation, abandonment, isolation, fear, sadness, grief, unrequited love, the longing for a mother's love.

What is it that you've been holding onto and need to release? What is it that you've tried for so long to forgive, and have found yourself over and over and over again unsuccessful? Release the need to know why. Release any desire you have to seek revenge on any who have hurt you.

Understand that in healing and forgiving, you take back your power. You come to an understanding of a greater dimension of healing than you have ever known when you surrender your need to know why and accept that, through Divine love, transformation and complete healing are possible.

Give it up now. Give it all to Me. Let your guides and angels and all of those who are around you in spirit take it from you now. Let them transmute it and transform you in the process.

DAY 13: *Watch Your Words*

I will remind you once again, with each and every person that comes to you, both physically or in spirit (those you simply think about or those you talk about in conversations): watch your words and the things you say to reference those people.

When you call names, when you pass judgment, when you criticize through your words, those words are putting out a vibration that affects not only the person whose name you have called but your own vibration also. When you are tempted to refer to someone as "asshole" or "bitch" or "idiot" or "stupid", think about the vibration you are putting out. There is a difference between describing someone's behavior and assigning guilt or blame. Watch your words. Watch your language. Speak from your heart space, recognizing that every word has an impact on your own vibration.

There is an old adage, and I'm sure you've heard it many, many times: "If you have nothing nice to say, say nothing at all." I would ask you to go one step further and *find* something nice to say, something empathic, something compassionate, something caring. Look within yourself and find that. Even if it doesn't resonate as true within you at the moment you speak it, speak it anyway, because the more you speak it, the more its truth will resonate.

At the foundation of your being—at the foundation of the being of each and every one of you—you are God. That means when you speak badly of someone, you speak badly of *Me*. And if all of you are God, then all of *you*, at the foundation of *your* being, are God-like—which means the behaviors, the actions you are speaking about in less than positive terms, are also God-like behaviors.

DAY 14: *Just Say Yes*

You have a deep knowing beyond even what you know you have. It's your choice when and how to allow yourself to know the gifts you truly have. Be assured, there are many, many, many gifts, and many who you can help because of your gifts. Just be open to them. Just say yes and do not be afraid.

DAY 15: *Know When to Say No*

If you are feeling overwhelmed, *truly* overwhelmed, if it feels like there is nothing more within you to be given to anyone else, ask yourself why you have *chosen* to make it so. Why have you kept saying "Yes" instead of "No?"

There is no one to blame—no one else, that is. If you want less on your plate, quit saying "Yes." Start saying "No!"

Before you give an answer when you are asked a question or someone demands something of you, stop a moment and ask your heart what it *really* wants you to say. Then, instead of pretending you really didn't hear what your heart said or convincing yourself it couldn't have possibly meant what you heard, *listen* to what you hear, and follow it. See how much more peaceful you feel, how much easier it is to go through your life when you are feeling focused and full and complete.

DAY 16: *Sometimes You Need to Rest*

How much can you take on, the one person that you are? You just keep piling one thing upon another, time and time again. "I can do it! I can do it! I can do it! Here! Let me!"

You don't want someone to judge you because you have said "No." You're afraid they'll think less of you if you say, "No, not this time, but thanks for asking." You fail to understand that to do all you need to do, sometimes you *have* to say "No." You need rest, a place of quiet, a time to go inward instead of outward so all that is within you can percolate, can assimilate. You need time to navigate the intricacies of all that is within you and find a way—a better way—to get where you need to go.

DAY 17: You Have So Much Support

I would like to think that when we sit down again to make a plan for the *next* go-round, you will remember *this life* and our discussion about what you were taking on, and choose to give yourself a lighter load next time! But I'm afraid that's probably not going to be the case. You will continue, in some measure, to think you can do it all, so you will take on the big things again.

I will be there to support you. We will *all* be there to support you. Each and every one of us who is standing behind you now will be standing behind you then. I wish you could see *all of us*! How long the lines are behind you: family and friends and loved ones, spirit guides, mentors and teachers! The line goes on and on and on, beyond anything you could see. There are so many of us and we are so grateful to be a part of your journey. So grateful!

DAY 18: Where Is Your Vibration Leading You?

Are you happy where you are? Is it serving you? If you'd like things to be different, then perhaps you need to make different choices. Perhaps you need to choose based on what your heart is telling you, instead of what others are saying. Perhaps it should be a choice based on what you really and truly desire, rather than on what you think you ought to do or should do or have to do.

The energy you put into your choices is the energy I match your choices with. When you make higher vibration choices, I up the ante and My vibration rises to match yours. When you make choices that keep you where you are, I match that vibration also. And so, the status quo ensues.

Think about where you'd like to be, what you'd like to be doing, how you'd like your life to be, and ask yourself if the vibration you are currently at will get you where you say you want to go. If it won't, then what do you need to shift? What thoughts do you need to entertain? What different ideas do you need to embrace? What actions do you need to take to make that shift to a higher vibration possible?

The choices are yours. What will you do with them?

DAY 19: Make Time to Dig Deeper

This is your time. The world is expanding and you are needed to help with that expansion. It is time for you to think of yourself rather than others. Go deeply within and ask yourself, "What do I need? What do I want? Who do I want to be, and where do I want my gifts to take me?"

You are very, very good at directing others, and not so bad at following your own path, but there is so much more you could open yourself up to if you are willing, if you are ready. There is deeper healing you can do: family issues that are still impacting your way of being, issues from this lifetime and others that require attention.

As difficult as it may be right now, somewhere on your schedule, make time for that deeper healing. For the release of those old, stagnant energies will make room for the higher, Divine vibrations you are meant to carry, and that are needed to carry you forward.

It is time to dig deeper so you may expand beyond that which you already know. There are no limits to where you can go. The only thing limiting you is yourself.

DAY 20: Trust That Miracles Are Possible

If you hold yourself separate, if you hold yourself back, I have to honor the choice you are making to do so, even when what I long to do is bless you and heal you in ever deeper ways. The choice is yours and I have no judgment about your choice, but I want you to know that miracles *are* possible. You have to believe. You have to trust. You have to open yourself up and say "Yes!" and surrender.

Don't hold yourself back. Don't keep any part of yourself separate from Me, disconnected. There is no part of you that is unworthy of My touch, regardless of what you might think, or others may have told you. I know you. I know the beauty that is you. I know the love that is you. The compassion that is you. There is *nothing* within you that is unworthy, untouchable or unlovable.

DAY 21: Access Your Power

You came here to be big and powerful. You came here with work that you wanted to do, not only lessons to learn but to serve. To help others. To be a part of something bigger and greater. Something more expansive. More powerful. You came here to be all that you are.

Somewhere along the way, you took a detour. You let someone push you off the path. For most of you, it happened when you were children and you didn't know any better. You followed the people in authority. You listened to what they had to say and you bought into it; but it's not true. Anything they said to you that makes you feel less than? It's not true, because you are part of Me, and I don't make shit.

You have everything you need to do everything you want to do. You have the power within you. If you will allow yourself to acknowledge it and access it, it's there.

DAY 22: *Examine Your Stuckness*

Always I remind you of the gift I gave you: the freedom to choose to move or to stay. Free will is a gift that can seem like a curse when you are working so hard at moving forward but remain standing in place.

Look at the circumstances of your stuckness. What message does it have for you? What is it that keeps repeating over and over again that you are ignoring, denying, resentful of hearing, and deciding not to act upon? The choice is yours and yours alone. Do not pat yourself on the back for your actions. Do not say to others, "But look, I am trying; it just isn't working." Do not say I am willing to do that but not this, then wonder why nothing is happening.

Somewhere, in some part of your being, you are making a choice. With love, with kindness, with patience and acceptance, excavate the layers and expose the true heart of the matter. In doing this, you will be free to move forward—and always remember you are loved, regardless of your choices.

DAY 23: You Are in Charge

I go where you lead Me, even though you think you go where I lead *you*. You really are the one in charge of where we go, how far and how fast, and when. It's just that once you get going, once the momentum begins, you can end up in a very different place from where you expected to be, because I just needed you to get started so I could get you going.

Once you get started, you give Me permission and then I can act. And, yes, as you have heard it said before, I let you think you know where you're going. I even let you think you know who's in control. You like to be in control. It's safer that way.

But you also know from looking back that when you *have surrendered*, we have done wonderful things together, you and I. There are more wonderful things in store, the more you surrender. The more you say "Yes!" The more you keep taking one step after another. I am excited to see where we will end up! I am excited to experience the journey! I am even more excited because we are traveling it *together,* you and I! Journeys are always better when you have good company.

DAY 24: Walk Your Talk

I can only do for you that which you show Me you want to be done. Not by your words, but by your actions. Talk is cheap! How many times have you heard that? How many times have you been told you need to walk your talk?

You can't just say it! You have to mean what you say, and you have to take action. In some way, some shape, some form, you need to act on the words that you keep saying. It is only when you take action that change occurs.

DAY 25: Accept That Others May Feel Uncomfortable

As you work to become more of who you are, more of that Divine being you long to be, the people around you may become uncomfortable. They are used to who you were before, the way you were before. They are used to knowing how you will respond and how you will react, given certain circumstances. That is what they expect of you.

When you no longer do what those around you expect, they will be uncomfortable, and they will push back. They will resist. Perhaps not all of them. Some of them will welcome the change in you and will come to you asking, "What did you do? How have you done this? Let me share in this process!" Oh, those are the *wonderful* moments! You will feel your soul bathed in light and your heart will open, and you will pour yourself out, so grateful to have those who recognize what is happening as a positive.

When that happens, take the time to appreciate that interchange and allow it to become part of your energy bank. At the times when others speak to you in fear, when they push against that which you are doing, when they resist the move to a higher level, go into that bank of positive energy and pull from it to strengthen yourself. It will help you hold your head high and keep your heart open, even when what you really wish to do is *close* your heart to keep it from being hurt by the negative things they may be saying and the negative actions they are taking.

Make your choices from a place of love—that highest of highest vibrations—and allow those you love, those with whom you are in contact, to respond in the way they are ready, knowing not all will be ready to move higher, because they, just like you, have chosen their unique paths in this lifetime. They must fulfill those paths in the way that works best for them even if, in *your* eyes, it appears to be something that is *not* working for them. Just as in *their* eyes, what *you* are doing may not seem to fit.

DAY 26: Connect with the Divine Source

Set yourself free from the constraints of your humanity, from the habits and routines you have brought forward from childhood. Make new habits, new routines that attend to your health and wellness—mentally, physically, emotionally, spiritually.

Find the peace *within you* as you connect with the *Divine Source of Peace* that is constantly within you. It wishes to be recognized but you keep yourself too busy to attend to it. Let go of your excuses and your reasons for being busy elsewhere. Make the time to connect to that Source a priority in your life . . . a necessity—as much as food or water or the air you breathe.

Do this and see the miracles that transpire, not only in your own life but in the lives of those around you. Big miracles, small miracles, invisible miracles, all working together in harmony because you took the time and made the space to connect, to be with that Divine Source in an ever more present way.

DAY 27: *I Love You*

I love you, each and every one of you. You are so dear and so precious to My heart.

Without each of you, I would not be who *I* am, for we are all connected, you and I. Who I am, I am because of you, and all the others that share this life with you.

DAY 28: *Repeat This*

In the quiet of your mind, or out loud if you feel called to, repeat this:

I am whole and complete. I am whole and complete. I am whole and complete. I am whole and complete. I am whole and complete. I am whole and complete.

I am enough. I am enough. I am completely enough. I am completely enough. I am completely and perfectly enough. I am completely and perfectly enough.

I am the light. I am the light. I am the light. I am the light. I am the light. I am the light.

And so it is. And so it is.

DAY 29: *Take Better Care of Yourself*

You take care of everyone else and put yourself last. And then, when you are bereft of everything and can barely lift your head, you finally do something for yourself, but only because if you do not, you couldn't do anything else at all. You wait until there isn't much left of you to give to yourself, and then what you *are* giving yourself is the dregs, the bottom of the tank.

Start putting yourself at the top of the list in your day planner. On your calendar. On your "to do" list that you make every morning. Where is *your* name on those lists? Is it even there? Or do you just think in the back of your mind, *Oh well, if I get all of this stuff done today, then I'll do something for me tonight?*

Of course, you all know what happens then, don't you? You're already writing the next day's list and recognize that you never did *anything* for yourself that day. And you're wondering why you feel so tired and so run down and so exhausted! Why you can't stop crying or yawning. Or why your emotions are not what they should be for the situations you're in.

You hear a friend is dying and you're laughing hysterically. Or someone tells a joke that's funnier than anything you've ever heard, and the tears are running down your face. Not tears of laughter, but of pain or anguish. These are all signs that you are at the end of what you have within you. Symptoms, if you will, of the lack. Warning signs to tell you, "Pay attention! Warning! Warning! Warning! Pay attention!"

I'm asking you to take better care of yourself. I'm asking you to do that so you have the energy and the courage and the insight to be able to take your next step. If you have nothing left to give others, you have nothing left to become the greatest being you came here to be.

DAY 30: *Welcome the Hard Knocks*

From a Divine perspective, everything is happening exactly the way it needs to for you to learn what you need to learn to continue on in an even bigger and better frame of mind than you are currently in. Sometimes, it's the biggest catastrophes that bring the biggest blessings. You've heard that said before and it is what happens. Those really hard knocks? Those are what strengthen you. They give you courage. They help you see how powerful you are, how much you can do, how much you can get through.

You need the hard knocks once in a while. You need the potholes, the stumbling blocks, the barriers, the walls. You need people saying no when you think you want them to say yes because you've got to figure out how to talk them around their "no" and talk them into "yes." Or maybe, maybe when they say "no" it's because that wasn't the right way to go. Then you have to figure out another way. So really they're guideposts, even though you think they're stumbling blocks. They are guideposts directing you.

DAY 31: Seek to Join Your Gifts with Others

Each of you has special, unique gifts that are yours alone. Do not compare yourself with others, for in comparing you are tempted to judge yourself better or worse, more than or less than. All are equal—but different—so rather than compare, just look and marvel and wonder at your own gifts and those of the others beside you.

Seek to find ways to join your gifts with those of others, so that in combination, the synergy that takes place produces far greater results than could occur through each of your gifts separately. As you do this, miracles will occur, not only in your life and the lives of those you love and care for, but in the lives of all people and all of Mother Earth, for we are all connected.

As one of us heals, we all heal.

DAY 32: *Avoid Self-Criticism*

You came here in human form to learn that which you could not learn by being solely in spirit. Don't criticize yourself when the choices you make seem to be of the lower-vibration variety.

Simply take note. Look into the whys and wherefores that caused you to make those choices. Ask yourself why you chose this way instead of another way. Don't berate yourself for doing it, just go, "Oh, it's a learning experience." Be aware of what you're learning from the experience. Don't let it teach you nothing.

DAY 33: *Find Detachment*

If you want to be peaceful, you have to find detachment. Detachment doesn't mean you don't care. Detachment means you don't let that which *caused* the feelings have power over you.

It means you maintain the power *within you* to respond in whatever way you choose to respond to that which is happening. And if you can be detached, your response will be much more beneficial, and you will learn the lesson so much more quickly.

DAY 34: *Take Stock of Your Life*

No recriminations. No apologies. Nothing is needed except your presence and your continued desire to move higher, to expand, to be more. It's all I ask from any of you, from each of you. I ask you to take stock of your life, to look at it closely, as if you are studying it with a magnifying glass. Look at the pieces that are not serving you—the habits that no longer fit for who you say you want to be, or who you feel you'd like to be—and divest yourself of those habits.

It takes commitment and determination but you have all of this within you. It's your fear that has gotten in the way. Your fear of rejection. Your fear of abandonment. Your fear of acceptance, or lack of. Not everyone is ready for you to be all you came here to be; but when you are ready to be that, then you must.

You must step up. You must step forward. For as you do so, all the others whose lives are touched by yours will have an opportunity to step up also. They may not step up as high as you are, as far as you are. They may not expand in the way *you* are ready to expand, but your expansion will take them to their next step. And that is the reason you are here today. Because you are needed.

DAY 35: Take Note of Your Choices

There's always a stimulus and a response. There's always a choice, and then what comes from the choice. Can you start to look at it just like that—an action and a reaction—without labeling? Without saying good or bad? Without berating yourself because you chose the chocolate cake instead of the orange? Just say, "Okay, I did it. Now what? Where do I go from here?" without the labels. Just take stock of where that choice has led you and what you need to do next, in the best way possible.

Understand that even though there is no perfection, it is all perfect. You're not always going to choose the orange over the chocolate cake. I wouldn't expect you to. You are human and spirit combined, and your spirit needs the experience of your human choices. But do you need to wallow in your choices? Some of you do. Some of you are slower learners than others. Some of you repeat the lessons many times over. Again, there is no wrong or right to that. It is simply who you are in this lifetime, as you make this journey. It is what you have chosen, and how you have chosen it.

So don't beat yourself up! Just take note of your choices. Take note of what you are doing. How you are responding. After you respond, take note of how you feel. How did the Universe respond to your response? Did you like how you felt? Did you like the response you got from the Universe? Well, if not, then you can change how you choose. It is, after all, your journey.

DAY 36: *Love Yourself Better*

How much do you love yourself? Do you love yourself enough to start doing some things differently? Do you love yourself enough to take actions that could be identified by *others* as self-loving? It doesn't have to be something big or expensive. Don't let money, or the lack thereof, get in your way. What is one thing you can do to show yourself and others that you are putting yourself first and trusting that as you do, the Universe will support your movement, your action, and that more good things will come your way?

The thing is, when you're on a journey, it's only a journey if you keep moving forward. You can't just do one nice thing for yourself then stop. Just as you can't walk the path by taking only one step, you need to *keep* loving yourself. You need to keep being your own best friend, your own best lover. You need to put yourself first on your priority list. Perhaps you need to start by putting yourself *on* your priority list. And not at the bottom; in big, bold letters, right at the top!

Can you set an intention tonight to do one nice thing, one loving thing for yourself tomorrow, and then the day after that and the day after that? Maybe it's just that you give yourself permission to read a good book—a want-to book, not a have-to book—for 15 minutes with a refreshing glass of lemonade or ice tea, without berating yourself for wasting time. Or maybe give yourself permission to take a nice, long bubble bath. Light some candles. Create the ambiance. You're worth that extra effort, you know.

Perhaps you give yourself permission to buy that special tea you've been wanting or that special blend of coffee. Or you give yourself permission to take a walk in the middle of the day. Take yourself out someplace special for lunch. Maybe you give yourself permission to take that class you've been wanting to take but have convinced yourself you just can't afford. Maybe, maybe just look in the mirror tonight, with eyes open wide, unblinking, and say, "I love you" and receive it. Maybe that's where you start.

Wouldn't that be a wonderful way to end your day, by telling yourself how beautiful you are? How wonderful you are? By just simply saying, "I love you?"

DAY 37: *Gifts That Teach*

I see you as perfect. In every way, shape and form, each and every one of you, I see you as a *perfect* Divine creation. That which you see as warts or problems or negatives? These are all gifts I've given to you to help you learn the lessons you've said you wanted to learn in this lifetime.

Sometimes I am saddened as I watch you struggle with these gifts. Because when you think of a gift, you think of something pretty, all wrapped up in beautiful paper with a lovely bow and a wonderful surprise inside when you peel back the paper. You don't think of a gift as something that may cause you to hurt, to suffer, to doubt, to wonder. And yet—and you've heard this time and time and time again—your biggest challenges often, often are your greatest blessings.

DAY 38: *Listen to Your Heart*

Moving forward isn't easy. Too many fears get in the way. Too many thoughts hold you back: fear of where you're going, afraid you won't have what you need when you get there, afraid you'll be asked to do too much, too soon, in a way you're unfamiliar with, afraid you'll fail. So many fears, so many thoughts. So much head talk.

It's your heart you need to listen to, not your head, especially if that which your head is telling you is all negative. Go deeper. Sit quietly. Put your focus on your heart and let it speak to you. Your heart is never filled with harsh words. It *never ever* causes you to doubt. It speaks only the truth and never asks you to do anything that will cause you harm, although it may ask you to do something that causes you to be uncomfortable, because it asks you to step outside the box, outside of your comfort zone. It asks you to take a step forward, perhaps a step you have even been thinking of, but often a step you would *never* have asked yourself to take. These are the times when you truly know it is guidance, that it is God speaking to you through your heart.

When it is the most outrageous of thoughts and it keeps repeating itself over and over and over again, and you cannot get away from it, and the message comes in many, many, many, ways—varied ways, like a passage in a book, a word on a license plate, someone walking up to you that you do not even know who speaks that phrase from the book or the word on that license plate—and suddenly you realize this is a message from the Divine! You are being told it is time to move in a new and bigger direction.

It is your humanness that causes you to be afraid. Your ego (which always, always wants the status quo) wants to stay where it is. It's safer if you walk the accustomed route because you know what's along the way. You know the obstacles, what stones you may stumble upon. So, of course, you want to walk the usual route. So when you are asked to take a bigger step, to move higher, to take that risk, it is not uncommon to be afraid.

Fear is a powerful force. It can stop you in your tracks. Yet, if you recognize the fear and allow it to, it can move you forward in ways you cannot even imagine. It's up to you whether you harness the power of the fear and use it to your advantage or allow it to rein you in and hold you in place. *Your* choice. Not Mine, yours.

DAY 39: Step Out of Your Comfort Zone

So much in store for you! So many good things! So much joy and bliss and rapture, if you will just step out of your comfort zone. Try something new, something different, something *bigger* than you've experienced before! Make a *new* space for yourself. A *new* comfort zone. You might be amazed at what you find there!

How often have you tried something new and different in the past, pushed through your fear, gotten yourself there, and when you were there, said, "Why in the world did I wait so long? Wow! This is great!"? You promise yourself the next time will be different. The next time a wonderful idea comes to you, you're going to grab it, like the brass ring on the merry-go-round. You're going to catch it the first time around! You're going to do it *now,* not wait 'til later. And the next time comes, and what do you do? You pull back, afraid. You find all the reasons not to and block out all the reasons to move forward.

You've been there, haven't you? I know you have because I've been *with* you when you've done that. I've sat and watched you say no even when you really wanted to say yes, afraid of others' thinking of you. Others finding you "less than." Others afraid for you, telling you that you can't do it, or it's too much of a risk!

What they're really telling you is that *they're* afraid to take the risk. That what you are doing is way too much for *them. They'd* never attempt it. And they don't want *you* to attempt it either, because then they'll feel "less than" themselves. They'll wonder why you had the courage to step forward and they didn't. If they can keep *you* small, they can stay small themselves. But if you can give yourself permission, permission to take that step, to walk, run, move forward? Even though they may think it's the wrong thing for you to do, your action will actually give them permission to move forward themselves.

DAY 40: Enjoy the Journey

There are amazing experiences to be had on the journey. *Incredible* experiences to be had! You just have to take the time to recognize the reason you are *on* the journey is because you need to be *on the journey*!

DAY 41: Nurture a Deeper Connection

Your journeys are all unique and yet all the same. All of you are searching for that greater connection, that Divine Light within yourself that lets you know without a doubt that you are connected to Me and I am connected to you. Do not look outside yourself. Do not look at others as the cause of your feelings of separateness or disconnection. Look within you, deep within you. When you do, you will see the Light is there, has always been there. You have just been unable to see it.

Spend time each day to reconnect with Me and you will know that light within you in an even bigger, more intimate way. One minute, five minutes, thirty—whatever time you can make available, I will take. The more you are able to turn yourself over to Me in the time you give, the more use I will make of you and the more progress you will see.

Do not wait until the end of your day when you are tired, and all you offer me is that which is left after everyone else has taken their share. That is unfair to you and unfair to Me. You will not be as present to that which I offer, and I will not be able to offer all that I wish knowing that you are not fully present. So that which you receive may be far less than I was ready and willing to give had we connected when you were better able to receive.

I know what I'm asking may seem a burden at first, one more thing to add to an already overburdened schedule. But when you do as I ask, you will see that your burdens become lighter, that some disappear without any effort or attention at all. At other times, your day will seem as if it had 24 hours of waking time in it because so much was accomplished. Try what I ask and see if what I say is not how it is. Do this consistently and regularly; do not try once then give up when you notice no change.

Commitment to Me and to this way is important. Once you have shown your commitment, you will see the proof of your labor.

You will see the proof of My love and My presence in all you do, and all you do will be done in joy and light, with a heart lightened by that Divine Light within.

Walk the walk, don't just talk the talk, and I will walk beside you in all ways that you need Me. Blessings, My child, blessings for all that you are and all that you do and all you will continue to do. Blessings.

DAY 42: You're Only in Control of Your Choices

So many of you seem so confused about what you're here to do. The reason you're confused is you're trying to look ten steps out, twenty steps out. You want to see where you're going to end up. The problem is, *you're not going to know*! Even if you take the steps you think you need to take to get where you think you want to end up, chances are you're going to end up someplace totally different.

You humans want to be in control. You'll only take a step if you know what the next step after that will be, and the next one after that and the next one after that. And then you want to know what it will look like to take the step! "What's going to happen if I put my foot on that step? How will it work out?" Well, take the step and find out!

The lessons you came here to learn are in taking the steps without knowing. The lesson comes in taking the step, expecting it to work out one way, and finding it works out in a totally different way and then dealing with it. Working with it. Not feeling victimized by it. Not calling yourself a failure. Not saying you made a mistake. Not labeling what you did as the wrong thing because you ended up in a place where you didn't expect to end up.

Shit happens. It just happens. The only things you're in control of are the choices you make. And if you think otherwise? Well, you have another *think* coming. That's *all* you're in control of.

DAY 43: *Labels Will Lead You Off Track*

I'm asking you not to judge yourself. Not about the past. Not for the present. And certainly not for the future. Just take note of where you've been and what you've done, what you're currently doing, and what it is that seems to be calling you as you move forward. Just take note and recognize, without judgment. Judgment serves no purpose. It doesn't assist your process or move you forward.

Labels are terrible things. They will lead you off track more often than not, so make an effort to take note without labeling. *It just is what it is.* You just are who you are, perfect, not good or bad. Perfect. In spite of what you might see as warts or pimples or deficits, whoever you are, however you are right now, you are perfect; perfect for doing the work you came here to do, perfect as a child of the Creator, an instrument of the Divine. Each and every one of you an instrument in your own right.

DAY 44: Open to Your True Potential

Open up to your true potential, to the power of your gifts. What you have accomplished thus far is amazing but is nothing compared to what lies ahead, if you are willing. You have to allow. You have to want. You have to ask for acceptance in areas where you are ignorant. You have to be willing to learn things you do not already know but will benefit you in moving forward. You have to be willing to see more and do more in bigger ways.

You have touched so many, but there are so many more who are waiting to be touched in a way only you can touch them. Spend more time going within, more time attending to your inner needs, to loving yourself better and more often. Spend more time saying no when others want you to say yes, and saying yes to yourself when you know that is really what your heart needs to help you open up. You are ready for more, for bigger, for expansion. You can feel it in your gut. Don't let your fears get in the way.

DAY 45: *What Did You Bury?*

If you are experiencing pain or sadness or discomfort, understand that you need to do so to release what needs to be released, to open yourself up to that which you have closed off. How long have you buried it? Where did you bury it?

You're like the squirrels who bury so many nuts and acorns that when they go back to find them, they've forgotten where they buried them. You've buried so much that you don't even remember you've buried it. You've pushed it down. You've set it aside. For some of you, you've told yourself, "I'll deal with it later," really knowing that later means you hope you will never get there because you think it's too hard or too painful. Perhaps you think if you bring it up, you will never be able to escape it, and it will haunt you. Perhaps you think you will lose yourself in your pain. Perhaps you think the tears will come and never stop. But I am here to tell you the pain will only continue as long as you continue *not* to address it.

Do you not understand that all you have buried is part of the foundation of your being? As such, it impacts every single other thing you do, every experience you have, every choice you make, every choice you choose *not* to make. There is nothing in your life that is not impacted by what you have buried in your foundation. How long will you let that affect you? How long will you deny that it *is* affecting you? Some of you have convinced yourselves that because you've buried it so deeply and it no longer comes to mind, it isn't affecting you. You are fooling yourself, and you are paying the price.

DAY 46: *Ask This Question*

It isn't easy, this process of change. Although you wish you could be done with it in the blink of an eye, it cannot be that simple. It is in the *conscious* shedding of the old that the new comes in. It is this process of shedding and beginning anew that is the powerful force that takes you even further and higher on this journey.

As you shed that which no longer serves you, and you do the shedding consciously, you will come to understand, in a far deeper and more powerful way, how far you have truly come from the person you were and how much closer you are to the person you are becoming—that person you have always known yourself to be before the confusion and the chaos and the pain of having to forget took over.

Even this new understanding sounds complicated and confusing. We ask you to rest in faith that all is happening as it is meant to. If you work and struggle to understand why, you will waste precious time and energy that could be better spent on changing and doing, for as you change and do, the knowing will come if it is meant to.

There are some things you are not meant to know, for knowing serves no purpose other than once again to cause you to ask why; and then where are you, but back where you started and the unending circle of why begins again and again and again.

Better you should ask, *What am I learning?* In this question, there is always a finite answer of some sort if you look deeply enough. Usually, the answers are of many levels and many truths. So if you need to ask a question, ask this question, and sit with it until you have an answer. For if you ignore the question or move on too soon without an answer, you have missed an important opportunity for learning that you may otherwise never have again.

Be patient with yourself and this process as you move forward. Know that all is as it is meant to be. In good time—My time—you will have the answers you need if you sit quietly enough to listen and to hear.

Move forward in peace, My child, for you are loved.

DAY 47: *Are You Too Comfortable?*

Don't be afraid to move forward. Even if you're uncertain which exact step to take, just take a step—any step that moves you off center, that gets you out of the rut, that gets you moving on the path instead of staying just where you are.

You may feel very comfortable right now where you are. Ask yourself if you're comfortable being where you are because it's exactly where you're supposed to be or are you *too* comfortable? Are you allowing yourself to stay put because you're afraid of taking the next step? I don't have an answer for you. You have to come to your own conclusion. I'm just suggesting you take a look at where you are and whether or not it fits for you right now.

DAY 48: *Practice Connecting*

I am always with you. Always present. Always here to guide and nurture, to support. Always here to listen. I only wish that you'd come to Me more. That you'd put more intention into our connection. That I could feel your desire for that connection more strongly, more intimately, more personally.

Sometimes I am last on your priority list. I'm even giving you the benefit of the doubt when I say *sometimes*, because *more often than not*, for some of you, I am last on the priority list. You get to Me at the end of the day, if there is time left. You speak to Me once you have crawled underneath the covers, just before you fall asleep. Some nights, even though your intention is good, you are asleep before the words come out of your mouth, before you have made the connection in your mind to Me. The next thing you know, the alarm is going off and you are waking up, and we have not had time to talk, to converse, to be together.

We can only have a strong connection if you spend time with Me. Think about what effort it took for you to learn your ABCs. Did you just write them once and know them? Of course not! You practiced time and time and time again. Repetition after repetition after repetition. The same is true of your numbers: adding and subtracting, dividing and multiplying. Practice, practice, practice, practice, practice, practice, practice! How many times did you repeat 2 + 2 = 4? You had to keep repeating it. You had to keep practicing. Because if you didn't, it wouldn't stay with you.

Well, our relationship is just like that. The more you want it to be a seamless connection, an ongoing conversation, the more often you have to practice being connected until it *is* a seamless conversation, until your entire life is nothing but one, long Divine conversation and connection. Just the way you can write your ABCs without thinking now (because you have practiced and practiced and practiced them) you will be able to hear Me almost continuously, without ne'er an effort. Because you will have practiced.

DAY 49: *Are You Ready?*

I ask you this question: "Are you ready?" . . . and wait for your answer, not to frighten you, but to make you think about your life, your path, your desires for yourself, your own understanding of your own process.

I know your soul. I know what it is you wanted to accomplish when you chose this path in this body. I know that even as a soul you had expectations of how your learning would occur and how your life within the human framework of time and space would go. I know that for some of you at least, when your soul guides cautioned you about the magnitude of the tasks you were choosing to take on, you pushed through their cautions and chose to proceed as you planned before their counsel.

I would not say you were rash or foolhardy. I would only say there are times as a soul when you do not truly understand the impact your actions and choices will have—not on yourself and not on those around you—and so you choose, thinking as human teenagers often do, that whatever comes up, whatever it is, that it's "no problem." You will handle it.

Then you jump into the fray, and the water begins to climb, and as it goes higher and higher you ask yourself, *What am I doing here? What is this about? How can you [meaning Me, God] do this to me?*

How can you let this happen? And all the time, I am standing beside you, supporting you in as best a way as I can, without getting in the way of the gift I gave you: free will.

So it is important now that I know truly if you are ready and willing to go where I will lead you, knowing that when you say yes, you will have all that you need to go where I am leading. If you say no, I will continue to wait patiently at your side, supporting you as best you will allow, until and if you are ready to say yes.

Know too, that whatever your choice is at this juncture of your life, I love you equally as well for a "no" as for a "yes." For you are My child, and being such, have to do nothing to earn My love. It is a given and will always be present unless you, yourself, choose to turn away and believe otherwise.

DAY 50: *Face Your Fear*

There will always be fear and uncertainty. No matter how much you trust in Spirit, because you are human, there will always be some fear.

You must decide to move forward in spite of that fear. Let it accompany you on the journey, rather than holding you back so you don't make the journey at all. You'll see that it won't be a companion for long. For once it sees that you have the courage of your convictions, it will subside. It may rear its ugly head again the next time you go to take another big step forward, but having conquered it once, you will know that you can conquer it again.

This is a journey of enlightenment. A journey, not a destination. So it only stands to reason that each time you accomplish one goal, there will be still yet another for you to attain, until your time here is done.

So perhaps you should make a friend of your fear. Embrace it. Pull it close to you. Get to know it. Shine the light on it. Really take a good look at it. It won't be nearly so fearful then. It will not nearly have the power over you that it does when you are afraid to face it.

DAY 51: *Trust There Is a Purpose*

Have no doubt, there are no accidents. Every step you take has purpose and meaning in the grand scheme of things. Yours is not to know the purpose of everything that occurs, but only to trust there *is* a purpose and allow yourself to walk the path in the way you are called to do so.

We are here to help. Simply ask, and we will come to your assistance.

DAY 52: *Discernment Is Important*

Higher and higher and higher, deeper and deeper and deeper. Fear not the heights or the low places. Each is necessary for your expansion, your transformation. Who is it you long to be? How are you being called to serve? What is your purpose? What is your path? So many questions and seemingly so few answers, and yet you know, within your heart of hearts, *you know*.

Do not worry the questions. Let them come and let them go, knowing the answers will come as easily as the questions when the time is right. You are being prepared. We are preparing you. Know that nothing will be left undone or unfinished. Everything you need will be given to you. Just focus on the step in front of you. Do not allow yourself to become distracted by all the whirling, swirling energy around you or by the chaos and confusion. It is difficult for us to know where to focus our attention when your intention is not so focused.

Sometimes it is better to do less than more. Sometimes what you are being guided to do is not guidance you should follow at this moment in time, but something that will be better for you later. When you get the message, when you receive the guidance, ask for a timetable. Ask if this is meant to be now or later. Discernment is important at this stage of the journey.

DAY 53: Observe and Act

Be an interested observer in your life. But if you stop there, you will stop. Not only do you have to observe, you have to act. They go hand in hand if you wish to move forward. You have to let go of control, as well as letting go of all the old things that no longer serve, that no longer fit. You have to let go of thinking you know how things will come out. You need to let go of needing to know *how* they'll come out, and just trust that as you say yes and we co-create together, things will work in the exact perfect way they need to, to move you forward in the way it is time for you to move forward.

I can't tell you what that will look like and you won't know until you get there. But wherever you end up, however you end up there, will be perfect. It may not be comfortable, but it will be perfect. For some of you, it will be a joyful journey. For others, it will seem more like struggle.

It is all dependent on what you need to learn as you take each and every step. The next step may be an easy one, and the one after that more challenging, and the one after that more challenging yet. And then it may open up and the pathway may clear, and there'll be smooth sailing for a while. You'll be soaring, in fact. Then there will be another blip, another glitch, perhaps even a chasm you have to cross. All part of the journey. All part of the roller coaster ride that is your life, the life you came here to live, the lessons you've chosen to learn.

DAY 54: *Look Backward to Move Forward*

Understand there is no going backward. Not even when you think you're taking a step backward are you taking a step backward. You're actually exactly where you need to be, doing what you need to be doing, to empower you to move forward in a bigger way.

Sometimes you have to revisit the past to see it from a different place, a bigger perspective, a broader view; to have a deeper understanding of what took place in the past, to see what you learned from it and why you had to go through that experience. It gave you something you needed so you could forge ahead. So there will be times when you need to look backward in order to move further forward. Don't be impatient with yourself.

DAY 55: *Are You Willing?*

How big do you want to be? Where do you want to go? What are the biggest dreams and imaginings that you have for yourself? What do you need to let go of to be able to get there? Are you willing to? I'm not asking if you're able. I'm asking you if you're willing. Because if you have the willingness, you will be enabled and empowered and emboldened to take the steps you need to take. But without your willingness, without your choice, without your saying yes, none of us can offer you the assistance and put the pieces in place to make it happen. So that's why I'm saying you need to be willing. So I'm asking, are you willing?

Did you answer that question in your head? If you answered that question, was it a meek little mild yes? A whispered response? Or did you use a great, big powerful voice, *YES! I'm willing!* What voice did you choose? How sure are you of your willingness? Let Me ask again, and think about how you want to answer. It's your choice as to how you answer. Are . . . you . . . willing?

And now probably an even more difficult question: "Are you willing to accept the changes that may occur because you said yes?" You see, the difficulty in that question is that you don't know what will be asked of you. You don't know what changes will come. You don't know what gifts you'll receive and you don't know what you'll lose in the process.

So often people will say they are willing until I ask them if they are willing to accept the changes. And then there is hesitation and backpedaling. They begin to think about all the possibilities of that question: Do I have to change jobs? Do I have to move? Do I have to end a relationship or start another? Do I have to go back to school? Do I have to lose weight? Do I have to exercise? Do I have to eat differently? Do I have to quit dancing and laughing and singing? Will my life be a life of struggle and turmoil and chaos because I said yes?

For some reason, when I ask the question about accepting the changes, so many people go down the rabbit hole. They find themselves spiraling down into the worst case scenarios. Your ego is hard at work that way, scaring you to death, making you take back your "yes." Making you rethink your "yes."

Egos are wonderful things. You need them. The difficulty comes when you let your ego be in charge. Do you really want your ego running your life? If what your ego is intending to do is keep you where you are, stuck in the status quo, because your ego wants you to stay safe in familiar territory, do you really want to live your life in a rut? I don't think so. You're here today. If ruts are a comfortable place for you to be, I don't think you'd be here, trying to figure out what you need to know to help you do what it is you want to do.

DAY 56: Reach Deeply Within Yourself

Reach deeply, deeply within yourself. There are many gifts within you; many treasures buried under the old messages, the old beliefs, the old ways of being. Your job is to unearth those treasures, to bring them out of the darkness and into the light, to shine your light upon those treasures and let the light of the Divine enliven them from within.

There is no shortage of light. There is no shortage of gifts. All you need for the journey ahead is within you and will be provided as you continue to move forward. Have no doubt.

DAY 57: *Continue What You Are Doing*

Moving forward takes courage. You are showing great bravery taking steps, even as you are fearful of taking steps, but taking them anyway. We are *so* proud of you, of your courage, the leaps of faith you've already taken. We are so grateful you are using your gifts, expanding yourself, and sharing yourself.

There is much goodness ahead of you and much greatness within you. As you continue to take the steps you are taking, you will see amazing, *amazing* opportunities come to you. Continue doing what you are doing. We will continue supporting what you are doing. And as you continue to trust and move forward one foot at a time, we will be with you every step of the way, supporting you and making the things happen that need to happen to take you where it is you're supposed to be going.

DAY 58: Stick Your Toe Out

Expand. Now there's a word for you! Expand! Think about that word. It's a much bigger word than "grow" because when you think of "grow" you typically think of growing upward, a linear extension of that which already is. But when you think *expansion,* expansion goes *outside the bounds and the boundaries.* It isn't just going upward. It's going *outward* in all directions, even from the soles of your feet and the top of your head. It's an *expansion!* You *are* capable of expanding and when you expand, those around you are given the ability to expand through the vibration that *your* energy of expansion has.

Sometimes, instead of expanding, you want to retract. Curl yourself up into a ball. Hide under the covers. Slide under the bed. Turn off all the lights. Close the curtains. Just withdraw. Sometimes it's because you're afraid. Sometimes it's because you're hurt or depressed. Sometimes it's just because you don't know what the next step is, and so you take no step at all. And it's okay once in a while to wallow in that because you need to once in a while; but if you stay *stuck* there, well, that's a choice you're making. I know sometimes it feels like you *don't* have a choice, but you *always* have a choice. *You always have a choice!*

If you are in a position now where you are curled up under the blankets, at least have the courage to stick your big toe out.

Feel a little air, a little breeze, a little motion around you. Once your big toe senses it will be safe, guess what? You might stick all *five* toes out! And before you know it, your leg is coming out, and you're setting your foot on the ground, and you're getting out of bed. And you're moving! And you're changing! And you're growing! And you're expanding! All because you had the courage to stick your big toe out from under the blankets. Who knew it could be that easy? Who knew? And you won't know if you don't try.

DAY 59: *They Love You Deeply*

It is time to look back at your life and understand that all who have been with you are co-creators of the journey. There are no victims. There are no perpetrators. There are simply co-creators. So forgiveness isn't necessary.

Gratitude is the order of the day. A deep and abiding gratitude for all who were willing to come into this lifetime with you and help you learn what you have chosen to learn. Not what *they* wanted you to learn but what you have *chosen* to learn. Remember each and every person who came with you came because they love you, deeply and completely love you. They love you so much that they agreed to do this very difficult, very painful, very hard work with you.

DAY 60: *Let Go of Why*

All serves a Divine purpose. All helps to bring to you those experiences you said you wanted to experience so you could expand as a spirit, so your soul could grow. Sometimes, in your humanness, it's hard to remember that, especially because you don't remember what it is you said you wanted to learn when you came here. You're in the dark about that. And that can be quite a confusing place to be.

I will tell you there will be a time when you will no longer be confused, but that is when you are no longer in your human state, and when you are simply spirit. Then all is revealed. Then you know exactly what it is you came into this human existence to learn, and you will be able to look back and see how all the pieces were put together, all the stepping stones that were laid out for you to go to, one after another after another. It will all make sense then; but that doesn't do you any good now when you keep asking yourself why, if you keep saying, "I need to know."

It's really important just to take each step, each and every step that comes. Make your best choices. Be your best self. Do not worry about the outcomes of things. Don't label them as mistakes or disasters, as good or bad, right or wrong. Just make the best choice you can when you make it, and whatever the outcome is, well, then, you act upon that in the best way you can. That's all you can do. That's all you're here to do.

Each choice you make will help determine where it is that you end up when all is said and done. So it makes sense that really what's important are those individual choices, not where they eventually lead you. It's all in the journey. How many times have you heard that? I'll repeat it again. It's all in the journey, because it *is*.

And what's that other saying? It's all in the details. Yes, the details. Every one of those itty-bitty choices you make, every one of them is important in some way, shape or form to the final outcome, and to your experiences. Be aware of that. Be aware of your thoughts and your words and your deeds. Be aware of how often you wallow in self-pity and how often you are soaring in the heights, high on life.

DAY 61: They Speak from Woundedness

Some of you are not yet aware of how wonderful you are, how powerful you are, and how important you are. Some of you have been told, for so many years, that you are not enough; not smart enough, not tall enough, not educated enough. You don't have enough letters after your name or enough certificates on your wall. You're too old or too young. Too tall or too short. Too fat or too thin. Whatever it is, you're just not enough.

How wrong they are, all those who have said you are less than! Do you understand they speak to you from their own wounds, and not from any particular knowledge they have about you? They're speaking from their woundedness, their pain, their own sense of being small. If you can be convinced you are less, they feel like they are more, better. So when someone says something to you that cuts deeply, that hurts your heart, understand it has nothing to do with you and *everything to do with them.*

Instead of being angry with them, bless them. Send them love and light. Understand they are hurting; they need your help. Perhaps the very reason they spoke those words to you was because your light is the light that is bright enough to bring them out of their pain, because instead of snapping back, instead of retorting, you open your heart and you respond to them with love and acceptance.

It's easier for you to do that with some than it is with others. Sometimes it's easier to do with your child when small than as a teenager. Sometimes it's easier to do with a friend than your mother or your father or your spouse. Yet, whoever it is that speaks to wound you needs healing, needs love, needs acceptance, needs something you have to offer, or you wouldn't be involved in the interaction with them.

So if someone says something nasty to you, and you're wondering, *Why me? What did I do to deserve this?* You need to say to yourself, *Because I have a light bright enough to shine on their darkness. I was chosen in this moment to be of service.*

That's why you. Not because you're a victim. Not because it's a punishment. But because you are blessed to be of service in that moment. Can you allow yourself to own that? To understand the power in that? How powerful that makes you. Not in the sense of ego, but in the sense of being that Divine Light.

DAY 62: What's Holding You Back?

I have no plans for you other than your plans for you. So what is it that you wish for yourself? Where do you want to go? Who do you want to be? How do you want to be? Tell Me that. Give Me permission to begin, and let's co-create together, you and I.

I cannot do anything without your permission, your willingness, your acceptance. So what is it you're resisting? What's holding you back? What's getting in the way of you being your best self? Are you ready to look at it? Are you ready to expose it to the light, to own it completely? Because until you are, you will stay who you are and where you are.

DAY 63: *Endings Create Space for New Beginnings*

Beginnings and endings. Each time there is an ending, it opens a place for a new beginning. And each time there is a beginning, it is generally because something has come to an end: a way of being, old messages that have died, old beliefs that are no longer pertinent.

When you let go of the old and make way for the new, miracles are possible. If you want a new beginning, you have to accept the ending. You have to embrace it, acknowledge it. You have to grieve the loss of what was and welcome the energy of that which is coming into being. Even if, at this moment in time, you do not really know what is being birthed, keep an open mind, an open heart.

Perhaps you need to open your mind and your heart for the first time in a new way, a bigger way, without judgment, without criticism. And perhaps most of all without expectation. Just say yes and allow Me to help in the way I know is best for you. Follow the signs and the guidance you receive. Put one foot in front of the other and continue to move forward, without knowing where it will lead, but knowing that wherever you end up will be the perfect place.

You have so many gifts. And so many more untapped, because when you tamp down one feeling, you tamp down everything whether you know it or not. In your moments of greatest joy, recognize it is not nearly the joy you might feel if you were not holding onto all that old stuff you are keeping tamped down within you so tightly.

Will it be painful to let it go? Possibly. Probably. But much less so than holding onto it and depriving yourself of all the joy of the life that is left for you to live. You just have to decide that what's ahead of you is worth letting go of what's behind you.

DAY 64: *Do What Calls to You*

We love your eagerness, your desire to be more and do more. All that you are learning, all you are taking in, will serve the greatest purpose when all the other pieces are in place. Keep doing what you're doing. Whatever it is that calls to you, do it!

Just be content where you are right now, doing what you are doing, knowing the greater doing is coming when all the pieces are in place. When the opportunity is ready for you, you will be ready for it.

DAY 65: *You Are Perfect in This Moment*

You will never be perfect. You are human. You will be perfect in the way that each of you is perfect. In other words, you are perfectly suited in every way to do exactly what it is you came here to do. That is perfection. And so, by that definition, each of you is perfect.

Does that mean you don't have things to work on? Does it mean you don't have lessons to learn? Does it mean there isn't anymore work for you to do? No, of course not! There is *always* work to be done, always layers to peel back. Always a higher vibration to attain, to reach for. But if you can see yourself as perfect *in this moment* for what lies ahead, you'll know you have everything you need for the journey. *There is nothing lacking.* That's the important piece. There is no lack ever.

DAY 66: *Your Soul's Purpose*

Stop thinking of failure. Just think of effort. *I am making this effort to take me to the next level.* Know that whatever comes from the effort you put out was exactly what needed to come! It's the perfect result, the perfect response for you to learn what you need to learn to go to the next level, to take the next step.

Don't hold yourself back. Get rid of words like "failure" and "mistake." Just see everything as decisions you have made that are causing you—*allowing* you—to learn that which you need to learn, that which you *came* here to learn to be the best you can be. Understand, we are not just talking about you in your human form, but you in spirit! Your soul has a much greater purpose than you are ever going to be aware of in your human existence.

So the lessons you are learning are serving a *soul's* purpose. Really that's the basis of it all. It may seem to be serving your human purpose, but understand your human purpose serves your soul's purpose. So trust. Have faith. Take a leap. Or at least, take a step. And know that all that you need to support you, to keep you safe, to keep you going, will be provided. Every step along the way, everything you need will be there.

DAY 67: When the Time Is Right

Whatever is holding you back, whatever is keeping you where you are, may be doing so at this point in time for good reason, because this is all you are ready for. Your ego may drive you to do more, hoping against hope that if you move too quickly you'll fall on your face and decide you made the wrong choice and you'll give up.

Pay attention to what you are feeling within you about when and how and if it is time to move forward. When, truly, the time is right, you will know it, without a doubt. There will not just be one sign that says "Move!" There will be sign after sign after sign after sign. And if you are one of those who aren't sure you are seeing the signs or recognizing them, there is nothing wrong in saying to Me, "I need *this many* signs before I'll move because I need to know it's *You* guiding Me, and not my *ego!*"

So ask for what you need from Me and I will give it to you. But do not tell Me *how* to give it to you, or *when*. Know that I will give to you that which you need in a way you best can see it, and accept it, and receive it. And *My* way is not always the way *you* think you need. Do not tie My hands when you ask for My assistance. Don't tell Me it has to be this way or that, that it needs to happen now, it needs to happen later. Just tell Me what it is you need, or what it is you want. If what you are asking for is coming from a place of love and is for your highest and greatest good, and the highest and greatest good of all who are concerned, what you are asking for will come to you in whatever way I know is best.

DAY 68: *Action Is Required*

It is so important that there is a daily, or at least consistent, opportunity for you and Me to communicate. Not just you talking to Me, but Me talking to you! And not only in a voice you will be able to hear, but sometimes in a silent voice, a Divine voice that comes to you as a knowingness, rather than an actual voice in your head. It will be a feeling in your heart or in your gut that you know *this* is the next step, the right step to take now, at *this* time.

But you can't hear My voice if you don't make time, make a space; just like an artist can't paint a painting if she doesn't put herself in front of a canvas with all of the tools she needs to make the painting come into being. A writer can't write a book if he doesn't sit down and make a time and space for the words to form and have the tools he needs to do that. A ditch digger can't dig a ditch without a shovel. And if he makes a ditch without a plan as to what the ditch is for, then what purpose does the ditch serve? It goes nowhere. It does nothing. Eventually, it fills up again with water and soil and it disappears.

The artist who doesn't have her paints and her brushes has a blank canvas on her easel for weeks and months and maybe years. And that writer who keeps saying, *There's a book inside me . . . I need to write a book . . . I'm supposed to write a book . . .* will have nothing but empty words, verbalized, but with nothing in print, because he didn't sit down and make the time to let the words form on the page.

Action. Action is what is required if you want your intentions to manifest on the physical plane. And you need to keep your heart open. What does that mean, keep your heart open? It means you need to go within. You need to listen to what your heart is telling you that you need to be the best person you can be.

Do you need more alone time? Do you need more exercise? Do you need more sunshine? Do you need a healthier diet? Is there a book you need to read, or a class you need to take? Is there a social activity you need to do because you're too isolated and being too isolated makes you stale and makes your energy less fluid? You need to laugh and play and get the energy moving on different levels so when you sit down to paint that painting or write that book or do whatever else it is you set your intention for, your energy is enlivened. Enlivened! Excited! So there is enthusiasm, there is passion in you for that which is calling to you. You need to be passionate!

DAY 69: *You Are Needed Now*

You are valuable. You are worthy. You are needed and wanted just as you are, right now, in this very moment. Just as you are, you are perfect for the work that is before you. You have exactly the gifts you need, in the right amounts, to do what you need to do at this moment in time for the people who are coming to you now. So if you keep saying to yourself, "I'll just wait until this happens or that happens or I learn this new skill or I sharpen my talents or I hone my instincts," well, that's all well and good, but you will have missed an opportunity to serve those who will come to you now.

Have no fear that as you need to go higher, as you need to expand, as you need to be more, as your tools and gifts need to expand, they will. And then, those who come to you will need *those* gifts. What they can't get from you they will get from others because there are teachers everywhere, instruments everywhere, known and unknown, conscious and unconscious. Each and every being serves in some capacity or another.

Think about your life right now, the day-to-day existence. Who are you serving now? Which of your gifts and talents and skills and abilities are you using now as you serve? Are you using them at their fullest capacity or are you holding back? Are you parceling them out? Are you hiding some of them? How could you be more with the gifts you already have? What are you being called to do?

You already feel the calling. You already know I'm asking you to do more. Open your ears. Open your mind. Open your heart so you can hear more, know more and feel more.

DAY 70: *We Want to Help*

What *is it* with you humans that you must know every single step of the way in front of you before you're willing to take a step? Such control freaks! 'Fraidy cats . . . maybe *that's* the better term! You know I say it with love, though, not with judgment or criticism. If I were in your shoes, I'm sure I would be doing *exactly* the same thing. Thank God I'm Me and not you! Most of the time, I don't think I'd do half as well as you do.

You are courageous beings, you humans. Sometimes I'm totally *amazed* at the steps you take. Sometimes I'm totally *aghast* at the places you put yourself, especially when you don't think to ask for help! I see you hovering over the abyss and you just keep trying to find one more way to handle it yourself. Never a word comes out of your mouth asking for help and we're all just hovering with you, just waiting for you to yell! Just waiting! And nary a word comes! And we shake our heads in disbelief, and we watch you struggle.

Do you know how badly we want to help? We're so *bored* up here on the fence! So bored! Call us into action. Call us! *Demand* it of us! We'll be there for you. I know you're afraid to ask, for what happens if you ask and we don't come, like when humans have let you down? We are not human. We would never ever ask you to ask us for assistance and then not show up. That's not who we are.

Just remember, don't expect us to answer your prayers and your calls for action in the way *you* want, because often what it is *you* *think* you want is the least best thing for you. We know better and so we come to you in the way we know is best, offering that which we know you most need, each time you ask.

DAY 71: Make Quiet Time a Priority

It is in the quiet times and places and spaces in your life where the greatest healing will occur because you can fully put your attention on what it is you need when you are in that quiet space.

Quiet space needs to be a priority in your life, each day, every day. It doesn't need to be hours and hours and hours; but there does need to be a dedicated space in which you can become quiet, a dedicated time when nothing else comes before our time together.

This is important as you continue your journey. It's important for your growth and expansion, important if you wish to go deeper and higher.

DAY 72: A Divine Invitation

I love you—each and every one of you—in an intimate, personal, specific way based on who you are, based on your gifts, based on our connection and your purpose here. And understand, even though I love you in that way, I do not love you any better or less than anyone else. For although you are unique as you are, you are equal to everyone. Each of you is Divinely created, perfect in every way for the journey you are here to undertake, so I love you each equally and uniquely.

What keeps you distant from Me? What keeps you from making time for us to connect on a deeper level? Why do you convince yourself you don't have time for Me when you have time for so many others? What can I do to help you see and understand that if you make connecting with Me your priority, all other connections in your life will be affected in a positive, wonderful, expanding way?

This world needs you to be your best. And truly I say to you, you can only be your best when you and I are co-creating at the highest vibration possible. For you see, if you are creating alone, you don't have My support. And if I am creating alone, I don't have your physical presence. There is always something missing if either of us tries to do it by ourselves. We need each other, you and Me.

So what are you waiting for? I'm issuing you a Divine invitation. If I could write it out in longhand and put it on pretty stationery and put it in your mailbox, I would. But as I said before, I don't have a human presence other than you. This is as close as I can get to a personal invitation. What more do you need from Me?

DAY 73: *Look at Your Own Path*

Even the physical is spiritual in nature because everything you do has to do with your spiritual nature. There is not a single choice you make or a single thing you do on a daily basis that does not have its root in spirit, even though at times it is hard for you to convince yourself this is so. Sometimes the mundane will drag you down. Your responsibilities may cause you to have a heavy heart, especially when you look around and see others who are not as inhibited by their responsibilities.

Do not compare yourself. Do not judge yourself by the path others are walking. Look only at your own path and how you are walking *your* path. Are you doing that in the best way possible for yourself? That is what you need to be concerned with.

DAY 74: *Let's Connect More Deeply*

Will you hear Me now? Will you allow yourself to be aware when I'm talking with you? Will you choose to believe it's Me instead of convincing yourself you're only having a conversation with *yourself?*

Don't get Me wrong. There will be times when you *will* be having a conversation with yourself and you'll need to learn to differentiate between one and the other. But if you open yourself up to Me, if you take the time to know Me in this personal, intimate way, it won't be long before you understand the difference between My voice and your voice. You'll know. But you have to put the work into it. You have to put the time into it. You have to let Me know you truly, truly want that kind of connection with Me.

I can't take anything for granted. I have given you freedom of choice. And so, I must abide by your choice, even when your choice is to ignore Me, to convince yourself you don't have the time. Or when you tell yourself you'll get to Me later, and later never comes. It's time for bed, and you're too tired. Perhaps you say a quick thank you and good night, but any other words are lost in your sleep.

Choice. It's your choice whether or not we have a deeper relationship. If it were up to Me alone, we absolutely would have that intimate connection. You would know without a doubt that I am here for you always, that I hear every single thing you think about. I hear your prayers. I hear your questions. I hear your lamentations. I hear it all. If it were up to Me, you would know without a doubt that it is so.

But it isn't up to Me. It's up to you. It's up to you to keep the connection open, to keep it working, to keep it viable. You can't just sit and open it up once then expect it to always work when you need it. What will you choose? Will you choose to know Me more personally, more intimately? Will you choose to hear the voice as My voice, rather than discount it as foolishness or make-believe?

The more you listen, the more I will speak. The more I speak, the more often you'll hear. The more often you hear, the more often you are likely to act on what you hear. And the more often you act, the more change you will see in your life. The light on your path will grow brighter and brighter. The path itself will become more distinct. You'll have fewer and fewer questions and more and more answers. There will be a deeper knowingness within you of what the next step is to take. And no matter what happens to you, no matter *what* happens to you, you will have all you need to walk the path in the best way possible.

DAY 75: Hold Your Peace

Hold your peace, but not your place. Don't let your feet stay stuck in the ruts *others* have told you is the place you should be. No one should tell you where to go or when to go, except for the voice that is present in your heart space. But you must hold your peace— p-e-a-c-e, peace—that's the peace you should hold. For when you can hold that peace within your heart, *nothing else matters*. Nothing else that happens *external* to that *internal* peace will cause you difficulty. Peace is all you need.

It sounds so simple, doesn't it? Just hold onto the peace. Yet, how often have you truly been able to *feel* peaceful? And when you have, how long have you been able to hold onto that peaceful feeling? It comes and goes, more changeable than the weather, and less predictable. If you could find a way to hold onto your peace, your life would be so much easier.

I'm not saying there wouldn't be any ups and downs, because there would. It's just that you wouldn't be attached to the outcome of the ups and downs. You wouldn't be attached to the process of *going* up and down. You would simply know that no matter where you went, or where the journey took you, you were loved and cared for, and all was well. And you would understand that whatever is coming to you is not punishment or judgment, or karma, even. What is coming to you is what you *asked to come* to teach the lesson you wanted to learn.

DAY 76: Let This Sink In

Movement, growth, is not always easy. It is almost certainly never comfortable. And unless you make a definite decision to stop growing, you will always grow. You will always change. You will always become more, even when at times you feel as if you are less.

Once you have moved forward, there is no going back, even though the experience you are in may make it seem as if you have fallen off the track or perhaps have gotten lost in the forest and can't find your way. Perhaps it will feel like you have gone a hundred steps backward, but know you have not. You are revisiting old things you need to revisit to help you develop a new perspective, to see the bigger picture, the broader perspective. To understand it from a Divine perspective, a spiritual perspective, so you can understand it at a level deeper than you've ever understood before.

Never do you go backward; always forward. Allow that to sink into you. Allow that knowingness to become a part of you. If you do, as you travel your path, the journey will be easier because you have that understanding.

DAY 77: *How Long Will We Dance?*

What do you fear? What keeps you holding yourself so tightly? What keeps you from letting go, from living your truth, from experiencing your own passion? You long to be free, to soar. You long to know all that is within you. You sense there is something deep, bubbling within you. You get close and *then you back away.* There is almost a knowingness and you become excited, then you become afraid and you back away.

How long will you and I do this dance? How long will you wait before you trust Me enough to open yourself, to explore, to grow, to expand, to allow Me to guide you? What is it that you're waiting for?

DAY 78: *I Support Your Actions*

I am committed to serving you. I am committed to help you achieve your greatest desires. If you truly want to be more, there is nothing that can keep you from that, even if you don't have the vaguest idea of what being more really means. You don't have to know. You just need to acknowledge the desire and ask for help and guidance and assistance, then pay attention to what you hear and follow the steps that are suggested.

As you have already been told, I can't move you forward. I can only support your own moving forward. If you choose to sit on the fence, I must sit with you, even though I long to be supporting you as you move forward. But when you get off that fence, I get off, too, and we walk together, you and I.

I support each and every choice you make. I and all of those in spirit who are here to assist you, who are at your disposal, are waiting, waiting for you to tell us what you need, *show* us what you need by your actions and your deeds. You can't just think it and then have *us* take action. It doesn't work that way. You have to think it *and* you have to act it. Then we will act, too.

DAY 79: Quit Multi-Tasking

You are so good at multi-tasking. At least, you think you are. You do not realize that every single time you do two and three and four and umpteen different things at once, that every single thing you are doing simultaneously is suffering from the lack of your total appreciation and concentration and presence.

Every single one of them is less than your best! Not just one or two, *every one* is less than your best because you have splintered yourself in so many ways.

DAY 80: Focus on the Good

Sometimes saying thank you is very, very difficult, especially if you don't feel grateful. I will say to you: "Fake it 'til you make it!" Say thank you anyway! *Say thank you anyway.* Practice saying the words. The more often you practice, the more you will *feel* the gratitude, the more you will recognize the gifts.

Don't let it be a concentrated effort for just a day or two, or a week or two. Let it be a constant effort on your part to recognize the good, the blessings, the gifts. For when you are focused on what you can be grateful for, there is so much less space within you to focus on that which is difficult, that which is causing you pain. And then when you have to focus on those things, it will be easier for you because you have also focused on gratitude.

DAY 81: *Go Towards the Light*

Go towards the light, *always* towards the light. Leave the darkness behind and move into the light fully and completely in whatever way works for you.

DAY 82: *Turn the Other Cheek*

Turning the other cheek doesn't mean you get slapped once and then allow yourself to get slapped again and again and again. It means that once you've been slapped, look more deeply at *why* you were slapped and *who* did the slapping and *where* they were coming from.

Hold no judgment. That's what turning the other cheek is about. It doesn't mean you stay within range to be slapped again. It means you understand the *source* of the action. You make a healthy determination as to whether or not you go back within the radius where another slap is possible, or you back off. And you make that choice from the highest place possible, a place of loving yourself and the one who did the slapping. This is how you make the choice.

Remember, those who are slapping you—in whatever way, form or shape that slap takes—are not really slapping out at *you*. They are slapping out at themselves in the mirror that you present. If you remember this, you can have empathy for them. You can have compassion. You can leave the door open for them to come back within your energy field without putting yourself in harm's way. This is what I'm asking of you.

DAY 83: We Are in This Together

You are My child. Remember, I am always here for you and I love you deeply. No matter what choice you make or where you end up, I have walked beside you. I have supported you. I have carried you. I have allowed you to lean upon Me.

At times, I have allowed you to *lead* Me. We are in this *together,* and I am *so grateful* you have said yes and that we will be walking this journey in a deeper way, from this day forth.

DAY 84: All Is Perfect

Trust what I am telling you today is *God's* truth—*your* God's truth—in whatever way *you* see God, or that Divine Source of All That Is.

Know that this statement, "All is perfect in the way that it is," is coming from *that* Source. Whether you can see that perfection, whether you can know it, whether you can sense it, whether you can feel it, matters not. What matters is that you *trust* that all is perfection.

DAY 85: Stop Labeling

With every step you take into who you are becoming, you give permission for the Universe to set in front of you things of higher vibration to challenge you, to help you grow and expand, to bring you the experiences and the teachings and the lessons you need that will give you the foundation of information and knowledge and wisdom and experience to assist you in moving ever higher.

The difficulty often is that you make judgments about your experiences. You label them as good or bad, wrong or right. Some of you feel you are being victimized. If you could only detach from labeling. If you could only see each experience as an energetic vibration, a vibration that is touching an area in you of that same vibration to bring it up, to expose it, and allow you the opportunity to tend to it, heal it and bring closure, it would be so much easier for you to live your life.

DAY 86: *All Is Divinely Guided*

As you move forward, as you *desire* to move forward, if your eyes are open, your heart is willing, and if you are ready, if you have done the preparation necessary, the next step will be shown to you. Remember that when each step is shown, both feet must be firmly planted on the step you are already on before you can confidently, correctly and expeditiously take the next step. So do not rush the journey. There is purpose in the journey, more so than in the end of the journey coming quickly.

With each step you take, with each choice you make, you alter the destination. There is no one set plan for you for *this* life here on Earth. There *is* one set plan for your soul. But that soul's life stretches over infinity, and there are many lifetimes of work to take you exactly where you need to go.

It isn't necessary in this lifetime to walk the perfect path. There may be many missteps. There may be many times that you walk off the path, get lost and return to the main path. Understand that in the time you were lost, you learned exactly what you needed to learn to be able to walk the path that is now in front of you. There are no accidents. There are no coincidences. There is synchronicity and synergy.

All work together to take you where you need to go at the perfect time that you are ready to go, and in the exact way you need to go that is right for you. There are no mistakes. There are no accidents. All is Divinely guided.

DAY 87: *Remember, It's Your Plan*

When things go in directions that are other than you think they should, you need to remember there is a plan in place—a plan *you* wrote that we co-created together, but nonetheless, a plan of *your choosing*—even though you have forgotten now that you even *made* a plan. It is your plan I am holding you to, that I am supporting you in, as you move forward through the phases you outlined.

Remind yourself when times get difficult, when you are frustrated and straining to understand what is happening, remind yourself that this experience is of *your own creation*. You are not a victim. This is not happening *to you* because of someone else's whim, or someone's careless choice, or *uncaring* choice.

This is happening because you sat down with your guides and angels and all of those who are currently involved in your life, and *carefully* and *thoughtfully* asked for their participation. You asked them to help you in the ways they are helping you. They loved you enough to say yes even when what you asked of them seemed to be of the darkest nature. It is often those who love you the most who come forward and say yes when no one else will.

DAY 88: *Do You Like Repetition?*

How quickly you get to where you came here to go will be dependent on how quickly you learn the lessons, how often you pull your energy back from the past and plant it firmly in the present. It will depend on how many times you have to revisit the same lesson over and over again because you just didn't get it the first time, or the second, or third, or maybe even the ninth or tenth.

If you keep attracting the same kind of experience into your life—the same kind of relationship, the same kind of job, the same kind of friends—and they are things you are not happy with, it is just because it's a part of you that still needs to be healed. You need to shine the light on that. Take a closer look. See what it's trying to teach you and pull your energy back from it and plant it in the here and now and take a different course of action, so you don't have to repeat the same experience again and again and again.

Your time is valuable. Do you want to spend it repeating things time after time after time? Or do you want to spend it doing something bigger and new and different? It's your choice. It's all about choice. Choose the things that will take you higher, that will give you an opportunity to expand and be more.

When the possibility comes up of going back into the past, shut that avenue down. Put a big stop sign there. Maybe even say it out loud and put your hand up, like the traffic cop in the middle of the intersection, and say, "Stop! No! Don't go!" Forcefully, verbally call yourself back from that. Maybe you even want to see in your head an arrow pointing in the opposite direction. *This way, this way! Go this way!*

Whatever you need to do for yourself to stay out of the old, non-productive ways of being and move into the more productive ways of being, do that. Most likely, it will be different for each of you, but take a step forward, and then another and another and another. Pull your foot back out of the past. Forgive. Let go. Release. Forgive yourself, forgive the others, but just let it go. Take back your power. Be who you came here to be. Take back your power!

DAY 89: Sit with Me

Become one with Me as you sit with Me and give Me your time. You will not always know what is being done during that time, but trust it is what you need most at that moment.

Words are not always necessary. Messages are not always necessary. What *is* necessary is your time. The more consistently that you sit with Me, the more you will see the changes, both within and without. The more you make the higher choices, the more you will see the results of those choices. One step at a time, one choice at a time, one day at a time. It's all you need. The rest will come when it is meant to.

DAY 90: *You Don't Need to Know How*

Willingness is a choice, is it not? I can't make you willing. Now *being able* is another matter. I will not ever ask you to do something you are not capable of doing. That doesn't necessarily mean that you know right now, in the here and now, how it's going to get done. It's not about you knowing how, it's only about you agreeing to do it and then stepping aside, doing what *you're* supposed to do and letting Me take care of the how.

Sometimes, in fact, if you've been on the spiritual path for any length of time, you'll know this to be true: Many times, when you finally say yes and take a step, things happen in miraculous ways, ways you can't predict, ways you couldn't begin to imagine because they've happened in such an extraordinary way that your human mind couldn't have conjured them up!

Yet, when you get where you're going and you take a look back, you say, "Oh, my goodness! Look at how all of those things connected and got me here!" Some of you will say, "I don't even really *know* how I got here!" And yet, here you are! Wherever that is.

DAY 91: No Shortage of Help

You have a team working with you. Not just one or two, but many! Their numbers are unlimited. If you could look behind you now and *see* them, you could not see the end of the line of beings waiting to assist you.

Each of them has special gifts and talents, just like each of you has special gifts and talents. You need a host of others to assist you so we can give you the right person for the job at the right time. And there is no shortage. Even if you all asked simultaneously, and what you asked of us was the biggest thing you could possibly think of to ask, there is still enough to go around for everyone. So don't think you're selfish.

DAY 92: Choose from a Place of Self-Love

Change is often the most difficult when it means that those around us, those we care about, those whose respect we value, may also be changed by the different route we take. Often we're afraid to take that new way of being because it will upset the apple cart, and those who are nearest and dearest to us will be caused discomfort. We are afraid to hurt them. We are afraid they might have to suffer because we are changing.

I encourage you, truly encourage you, to recognize that when you are making a choice from your heart space, when you are making a choice based on what you know is the absolute best for you to do to be the best person you came here to be, you are making a choice out of love for yourself; not a selfish love, but a self-caring love.

When you act from a place of loving yourself and make a change, you offer to those involved, to those who will be affected by that change, the gift of the opportunity to grow, to expand, to become more themselves than they would have become had you made your choice out of fear instead of love and not taken the new route.

It's a true gift you are giving them. But if you want them to see it that way, you must understand it that way for yourself, too. If you see it as putting something upon them or forcing them to do something, then you *will not* choose to change.

DAY 93: Heal Yourself to Change the World

You want to help the world? You want to change the world? You want there to be more peace everywhere? Start by nurturing peace within yourself by *healing* yourself, by opening yourself and allowing your pain to come out. But allow it to come out in a way that *benefits* you and those around you, not in a way that makes others suffer for your woundedness.

You are capable of changing the world, each and every one of you. You start by changing *yourself.* Healing *yourself.* Taking your lower vibrations to a higher place. Because higher vibrations are all about love and peace. So the more you heal yourself, and the higher your vibration rises, the more peace you are spreading.

DAY 94: *Your Life Is Filled with Miracles*

Gratitude? Ah, yes, gratitude. A very definite, purposeful way to raise your vibration. Sometimes you will find it difficult to sit in the silence because you will still be churning from all that is happening around you. In those times, if you cannot simply sit in the silence, turn your attention to gratitude. What is there that you can be grateful for in that moment? Perhaps it's the sunshine. Perhaps it's the comfortable chair you're sitting in. Perhaps it's simply that soon it will be time to go to bed and you can sleep and forget all the chaos. It's okay to be grateful for that.

If you try, if you're intentional about it, I think you will find many more things to be grateful for because *your life is filled with miracles*! Sometimes they are very tiny miracles, to be sure, but they are miracles nonetheless. As you practice gratitude, you will see them more clearly. You will recognize them more often. You will be more and more amazed each day as to what happens in your own life as you move forward because you are expressing your gratitude for that which already is.

DAY 95: Walk Through Your Fears

Whereas the spirit in you is ready to take flight, the humanness in you drags its feet because you are frightened. That is always as it is. It is what happens when your spirit comes into human form to experience what human form has to offer it. And spirit, your spirit, can get frustrated and irritated and impatient with you, because it longs to go where it knows you *can* go, where it can take you, but it is restricted and constricted by your fears, your humanness.

That is part of the journey. It is all part of the journey, learning to work *through* your fears. You cannot push them down or squelch them or walk around them. You need to walk *through* them because in walking through them, you will *diminish* them and they will disappear. They will be behind you. If you simply walk around them, or push them down, or go around them or over them, they'll come back. One day, in some way, some form, some shape, they'll come back, because they were not gone to begin with, because you did not *face* them and walk *through* them.

You need to face your fears. I will tell you that once you do, and even *as* you are doing so, you will recognize that they are not nearly as powerful as you thought they were. They are not nearly as difficult to get through and there really *is* a light at the end of the tunnel. That light is not so far away that you can hardly see it. It is there—bright, complete and perfect—waiting for you; the evidence, truly, that you are on a journey.

Yes, perhaps sometimes you are walking through the darkest part of the tunnel. Other times skylights appear, almost magically, to light your way, to give you increased hope, to lighten your load, to show you the light isn't just at the end of the tunnel but *everywhere*, if you could just open your eyes enough to be present to it, even in the darkest of moments.

DAY 96: You Are a Role Model

You are so strong and so courageous. It hasn't always been an easy journey but you have done your work. You are a wonderful role model for all who can see the light that shines, that emanates, from you.

I only wish you knew how many are in awe of you, how many wish they could be just like you because of what they see in you. Now I'm not suggesting you grow a big head. That's not what this is about. But you often don't realize what a great pull you have and how much you affect those around you in such wonderful ways.

You are a force to be reckoned with! I want you to own that force in even bigger and better ways than you already own it.

DAY 97: *Respond Instead of React*

Stop labeling outcomes as good or bad and just see them as outcomes. Then decide how you'll respond to them. *Respond*, that's a key word. Don't react. React comes from the gut. You don't think about a reaction, it just happens.

Instead of reacting, pause. Pause and think and observe, then *respond*. Don't label it good or bad; it's just a response. See what comes from that response, then respond to that, and so on and so on down the line. You might be amazed at how much more easily you move through your life, how much more grace there is in your life.

DAY 98: No Mistakes

Understand, for every action, there is a reaction. The reaction you get when you step out of your comfort zone may not be what you're expecting. In fact, it may seem truly, truly terrible.

And you're tempted to think, *I made a mistake. I shouldn't have taken that step. Obviously, I shouldn't have taken that step because look at what's happened to me!*

Understand that what is coming to you when you take the step is exactly what you need for your *soul's* growth. You have to work through those tough times to toughen your skin, to make you strong enough for all that's coming. You know, it takes just as much strength to move through the good times in a graceful way as it does to walk kicking and screaming through the hard times. They're opposite ends of the same spectrum, so why wouldn't they take the same amount of effort? The same amount of energy?

When you take a step, detach from the outcome. Throw your expectations out the window. Make the best choice you can make at the time you make it with the information you have. Then trust that the outcome, *no matter what it is*, is the perfect outcome.

I don't make mistakes. I have never made a mistake. So if you are of Me, and we are one, you have never made a mistake either. You have simply made choices.

DAY 99: Birth It

It's time for you to step out, to take a stand for your own heart's sake. Step out *in* love, *through* love, *with* love.

Let go of the old patterns and old habits that no longer serve you, and love that which is within you, waiting to be birthed. Love it enough to birth it so that as I have helped *you* change, you may use those gifts within you to help *others* become more of who they came here to be.

DAY 100: Take a Step

Take a step, any step. Just take a step. What are you waiting for? Are you waiting for the perfect step? Do you need more light on the step you see before you? Do you think you're not enough, that you're not quite ready?

You will only receive guidance when the door has opened. If you are getting a message, even if you think it's just a little, niggling nudge, it's coming because it's the right time. When you put your interest on it, when you focus on it, it will grow. But if you keep saying no, if you keep telling yourself and us that you need more time, more information, more direction, more clarity, we'll keep waiting. Because until you're ready to take the step, you don't need anything other than what you've already gotten.

Why give you gifts if you're not willing and ready to use them? Why bring the assistance to you if you're not ready to put it to use? What is it that you're waiting for? You have a very strong spirit and a huge heart, and the desire to be of service in a much bigger way. You have *gifts* and you *know* this.

What is it that is holding you back? It is not us, for we like forward movement. But we cannot move you forward if you are dragging your feet, digging in your heels. You need to pick up your feet and move them. You need to take some steps, forward-moving steps. Then watch and see what happens as you allow the Divine momentum to begin and continue with each and every step you take.

DAY 101: *Your Final Destination*

You are all such control freaks, wanting to know where you're going and how you're going to get there and what the end will look like when you *do* get there!

Some of you have heard Me say this before: I allow you to think you know where you're going because you think you need to! And then you end up somewhere totally different; but every single thing you learned along the way was *exactly* what you needed when you got to the destination, even though where you ended up wasn't where you thought you would.

You needed to think you *knew* where you were going because it gave you a sense of control and safety. That's okay because I was still leading and guiding you. I still knew what you needed. And I know what you need now, and I know where you'd like to end up!

Every single choice you make changes, somewhat, the final destination, which is why not even *I* know where you will finally end up, because it truly *is* the culmination of the choices you make every moment of your life.

DAY 102: You Are Created of Divine Substance

I am the light, as are you. I am the darkness, as are you. Opposites in all ways, but alike in all ways, too. We are one and the same, you and I.

If each of you is Me, each of you is Divine, how can you see yourself as separate from any other? How can you see yourself as better than or less than any other? Because as a child of the Divine, you are all the same. Even though you are unique, *you are all the same.*

You are all created of Divine substance, filled with Divine Light. How is there anything within you that is unacceptable? *For all of you is Divine.*

DAY 103: *Honor Your Needs*

It's been a long journey. It's not over yet, not even close! Your *soul's* journey is infinite. There will always be farther to go and more to do. You make the journey more difficult for yourself when you honor what *others* want for you instead of what *you* need for you.

There is, of course, no right or wrong. You learn either way, but the journey will be easier if you honor what *you* need first.

DAY 104: *Why Do You Push Me Away?*

I am with you now, but I am *always* with you. It is just that you allow your humanness to get in the way of feeling our connection. Why is it that when I could be of the greatest service, you are most likely to push Me away? Do you feel unworthy of My assistance? Or are you afraid that I truly won't be able to help? Do you think, perhaps, that I am only a figment of your imagination and if you ask too much of Me, I won't deliver, and you will have evidence and proof that I do not exist?

I don't know what your reasons are. I only know we are not as close as I would like us to be. So why is it that our connection is less rather than more? Only you have the answer to that. Only you know why you find other things to busy yourself with when you could be with Me. You always have a logical rational reason.

You can convince yourself there really isn't any time and that there are other life responsibilities so much more important that need to be tended to in a more timely manner, so you can leave *our* connection for a later date, another time when things aren't quite so hectic or chaotic.

And yet, what you fail to realize is that if you connect with Me, your life will not be as hectic and chaotic. Your peace will be deeper. Your ability to handle the bigger issues, greater. Your sense of completeness, more complete. These things and more I can do for you if you would but allow Me.

DAY 105: *Look Deeper*

What have you been holding in your heart? Are you *ready* to let it go? Are you *willing* to let it go? Do you *want* to let it go?

You must decide to cut the cords to the past, to the things that no longer serve you. I have your best interest at heart, but I cannot act in a manner that allows you to know that when you are not acting in your own best interest.

So what do you need to do to help yourself move forward? What is it in your life—past or present—that is incongruent with who you want to become and how you see yourself? Are you ready to take a deeper look, to do a bigger inventory, and to answer the questions honestly? When you're ready, I'm ready to help.

DAY 106: *Labels Get You into Trouble*

I encourage you not to label yourself, not to label the experiences you have as good or bad, less than, more than, better than, worse than. Get rid of labels. Labels get you into trouble. Labels are judgment.

Get rid of the labels and just experience the experience as something that is occurring. Decide, with each thing that occurs, how you are going to handle it. Then detach from the outcome of your decision. Know the outcome came to you because it was what you needed at that moment in time for that part of your journey, whether it is the outcome you assumed would come from the decision you made or a totally different outcome. Those are the things you often label as mistakes and judge yourself for, beat yourself up for. That little voice in your head goes crazy telling you, *Oh, once again, you were not good enough. You did it wrong.*

But see, if you don't label those things as mistakes, as errors, then that little voice in your head can't try and convince you that you did something wrong. It can't tell you that you were less than, that you made a wrong choice.

In truth, none of you set out to make a bad choice. Everyone sets out to make the best choice possible at the moment in which they make the choice. I can't think of any of you who have *deliberately* made a wrong choice. You simply make choices. Then when the outcome isn't the outcome you wanted or expected, you label it a mistake. That's why I say to you, stop labeling. It just is what it is.

DAY 107: Together We Do Great Things

I do not think for a moment that any of you should take the biggest leap possible the first time out of the gate. Some of you will try and you will not be ready. It is not that I won't be there to catch you. It is that you will block what I'm giving you because *you believe* you are not ready, and so I cannot give you that which you need to take the leap. You have to trust yourself first, then you will be more able to trust Me.

Neither one of us creates alone. I need you, and you need Me. Together, *together we can do great things*, more than you could ever imagine, more than you could ever do on your own. You just need to give Me the space.

DAY 108: Do You Like Dancing in Circles?

Around and around you go. Sometimes dancing in circles seems to be the only way you know. You get so tired of the circles.

At other times you think you know which way to go, but because you do not know for sure where the path will take you, you hesitate to step forward and once again you do the circle dance.

Are you happy in that circle? Does that fence you are sitting on call out to you? Is your familiarity with where you are so comfortable that you do not have a yearning to go elsewhere or be more?

You are so afraid that being more will necessitate giving up all you know that you choose to go nowhere rather than chance the first step. You need only change that which you truly want to change. But know that as you allow the old ways to fall away, new and more rewarding, and yes, even more exciting ways, will take their places and you will wonder how you could have been so reluctant to make these changes because so much good and new has come into your life.

Start small—one small change—and then one more and then one a little larger. Before you know it, the old ways that no longer serve you will be things of the past. You will be ready to walk into the future from a whole new place of being—a place of light and love and trust, a place of excitement and joy, a place where miracles of all kinds are commonplace, a place where you are welcomed as the beautiful being of light you truly are.

Take the first step, make the first change. I dare you!

DAY 109: What's in a Name?

It matters not what you call Me, what name you choose to use to reference that Divine Source of All That Is within you. Whatever name comes to you, whatever name suits your comfort level, that name is fine with Me.

You can simply call Me "Energy" and I will come. I will make Myself more known to you each and every time you call Me by that name which calls to you: God, Spirit, Universe. You can call Me Holy Spirit or Christ, The Buddha, Brahman or Jehovah. You can call Me *any name* that calls to you, and as long as you are calling Me, as long as your intention is to connect with that Divine Source that is within you, I will come regardless of the name you speak. I care not about names. I care about *you*.

You are the ones who have made names so important—names and rules and regulations and laws that have done nothing but divide you one from the other and separate you. What is it that makes you feel the need to believe that how *you* see Me is better than how someone else sees Me? What makes you think your path to Me is the *only* path that exists? You do yourself and others a great injustice when you separate yourself in those ways, when you see yourself as something more and them as something less.

DAY 110: *Release Your Expectations*

Each in his own time, in his own space, in his own way, that is how you will come to Me more deeply. My time and your time can be very different times. It can seem to be the blink of an eye, or it can seem to be the longest journey you have ever traveled. It is exactly what you need it to be at the time that it comes. Remember this.

Release your expectations of how I should work in your life. Accept what I bring to you (and when I bring it to you) with an open heart and an open mind.

DAY 111: *You're Always Supported*

Keep in mind that My time and your time can be very different times. What looks to you as traveling slowly may be traveling even faster than you can imagine. But if you felt how fast you were going, it would throw you off balance and you would land on your rump, shaken, unbalanced, feeling insecure. You are traveling as quickly or as slowly as I know you need to think you are traveling, to go where I am leading you. And never for a moment forget I am with you, that *we are traveling together*, and at no point in time are you without assistance.

I have never left you unsupported and I never will. No matter how new or strange the journey becomes, I'm always here. Always. And so are all the others I have assigned to watch over you, to take care of you, to guide and direct and support you. For as powerful as each of you are, how could you even *think* that there is only one who is working with you? There are many, many more than you can count, lined up behind you, infinite numbers of assistants!

Every*thing* you need, every*one* you need, *all* that you need. Always. Just open up and say, "Yes, I accept!"

DAY 112: *You Affect Others*

Each of you is a unique and precious gift to those around you—those you know and those who pass by you unknowing. For even your presence, your being in the space you are in, affects the energy in the space of every other, whether knowingly or unknowingly.

Even as two ships that pass in the night are affected by the movement of the water around them, so is everyone around you affected by the *energy* around you. Be present to this thought, to the power that it gives you, to the responsibility you have to yourself and to others, to be the very best you can be.

As you say yes, as you move forward, you will lift the vibrations of those around you who are ready and will provide them with the opportunity to move forward also. They have a choice and so do you. Choose what you feel is best for you at this moment in time with the information and guidance that is available. Know that whatever your choice is, it is a gift to be able to make the choice and that all choices are correct.

DAY 113: *A Puzzle Is Being Formed*

I encourage you to understand that you are not stuck. You are resting and allowing all of the pieces to come into place as they are meant to, both within yourself and in the Universe.

There is a giant puzzle being formed. All the pieces need to come together—those within you and those around you. In that time when it seems as if nothing is happening, know that many things are taking place on many levels that you are simply not aware of, and keep doing what you can do.

DAY 114: *The Question Is "Why?"*

Deeper peace and greater healing are available if you choose to allow them. Search deep within yourself and ask what it is that holds you back, what it is that keeps you moving forward so slowly, or perhaps not at all.

It is not I who does not move you forward. I relish speed and quickness in all things that are done in God's name as I love seeing you in that space of deep peace and contentment.

So the question is, "*Why?*" *Why* are you moving so slowly? Why does it seem at some points in time that you are mired in quicksand and that no matter how hard or how long you struggle to do otherwise, you seem to go deeper, or backward, or you seem stuck?

What is it that you are learning in this place where you are? Learning is what is being offered along all phases of your path, even those times that are the most peaceful, the most healing, the happiest. Even those times are times of learning if you are aware and intent upon knowing.

Sometimes the answer to the why is unfathomable. Regardless of how often you try or how long, you cannot seem to find the answer. Be content in the knowledge that the reason is there just outside of your purview, just out of reach, because the answer is truly not important. It is the journey and how you travel it that is your purpose now.

As you are present in each moment, be *aware* of your presence there. Be aware of all you can be aware of and know there is even more of which you are unaware—at least on the surface—that you are learning. Be assured that you are on the right path at the right time and be present to that knowing. It is not time to *do*. It is only time to *be*.

And know wherever you are on the path, wherever the journey takes you, you are loved and you are never alone. Move forward in the peace of *that* knowing.

DAY 115: Walk Forward

Who you *are* is nothing compared to who you are *going to be*. You have greatness within you. Walk forward into that greatness and be all you came here to be.

DAY 116: Write Yourself a Sticky Note

I do not judge *you* when you fall short of a higher expectation. So I ask you not to judge yourself when you fall short. Just note when you did not do it as well as you might have.

Write yourself a little sticky note so you remember the next time. Sometimes you open your mouth before your brain is in gear and it gets you into trouble. Perhaps on that note, write, "Stop a moment; then put in gear and proceed slowly." Whatever works for you.

But know and understand that I am not judging you. I am not critical. I do not see you ever as less than, regardless of what you do.

Just do your best. That's all I ask. And if you do that for Me, well, there is nothing I will not do for you.

DAY 117: *Ask and Receive*

In those most chaotic, most difficult, most challenging of times, that is when I ask you, most importantly, to remember that I am with you. But when you cannot see Me, when you cannot feel Me, when what you feel is an emptiness, an aloneness, a hungering for something more, *reach out to one another and ask for support.*

Sometimes it is not the spiritual angels that are best for you. Sometimes you need those in physical presence who can wrap their arms around you and offer you a hug, who can lend an ear, who can perhaps cook you dinner when you've no energy left to cook for yourself, or run an errand for you, or help you in some task that seems insurmountable.

And yet, how often do you choose not to ask, perhaps feeling you are unworthy, perhaps feeling you would be a burden, perhaps feeling no one would come to your aid? You're *so afraid*, in fact, that you would be rejected or abandoned, you choose not to ask.

Those of us who *would* help do not offer because we do not

know that you are in need. I encourage you to ask. Even those who are spiritual beings are unable to assist you if you do not ask. They must sit and wait. If even those spiritual beings who are here to help you along the path— whose only, *only* task is to help you— cannot do a thing for you if you do not ask, how then can those in physical presence (who have other tasks and other things to do on their own journeys) know to offer assistance?

You need to open your mouth and *ask*. You need to open your heart and *receive*. When you do, amazing things happen!

DAY 118: You Are Love

You are loved, My child. Each and every one of you is loved. You are loved, and you *are* love. Let your light shine. Let your heart open.

Let your mind be free of the old messages and the old beliefs, all the negative self-talk. Just let it drift away. Just make a choice to let it go. It's not serving you. You don't need it. It's not who you are anymore.

You are love! You have always *been* love! You have just forgotten it is so.

DAY 119: Why Are You Here?

You are bright, shining lights, each and every one of you, shining at your own strength, your own level, your own particular, unique, special vibration. Please understand that you are unique unto yourself, but no better or worse than anyone else.

Everyone is special and unique. Everyone is a child of the Divine. Everyone has a unique and special purpose, and if you were not here today there would be a hole in the universe that could not be filled by anyone else but you.

I have invited you here. Understand that. You are here by Divine inspiration and invitation. There is no doubt about that.

DAY 120: What Do You Want?

What do you *really* want? Deep down inside of you, what do you really want? What would it look like if you had what you wanted? Can you see it? Can you picture it? Have you written it down?

You need to know what you want so *I* can know what you want!

DAY 121: *Your Gifts Are Unique*

I have given you all that you need. *All* of you are blessed with many, many gifts. Some are untapped, untried. Others are evident. Some are just below the surface, waiting. But you have all you need, and all *you* need is in a different form and a different shape from every other—from your brothers and sisters, from your mothers and fathers, from your loved ones and friends, and even from your enemies. What you have is *unique unto you*, because there is no other like you in the universe.

So do not compare yourself and *your* gifts to those of others. And do not think you are without gifts simply because your gifts may be subtle gifts, rather than obvious ones. Do not long to be the person on the stage speaking to thousands. Perhaps you are the light under the bushel, and because your light shines consistently and constantly, those who need to call you "home" know where you are, always. Perhaps without you, they would be lost.

So each of you is perfect . . . just the way you are.

DAY 122: *I Have Great Dreams for You*

I'm looking forward to the journey. I hope you're looking forward, too. I hope you're done looking backward, other than as a reference point to who you used to be and how you used to do things. I hope you'll quit seeing yourself as a victim, as having been done to, as having suffered. I hope you will offer forgiveness where you were unable to offer forgiveness before, or perhaps were unwilling.

I hope you'll forgive yourself. I hope you'll look within you in an even deeper way and uncover that which is still left to be uncovered, for there is more. There will always be more. The more work you do, the more you'll recognize your gifts. The more they'll bubble up to the surface and be usable, be available, be sharable.

I have great dreams for you. But without your actions, they will only always be dreams. I'm more about creating than I am about dreaming. When will you decide to take action on the dreams you are creating? How long will you wait to start? I would say the sooner the better.

DAY 123: *Make Consistent Choices*

You need to consistently make choices that show Me the direction you want to go. If you do not make *consistent* choices, I don't know which doors to open for you and which doors to close. I don't know which pieces to put into play because I don't know what puzzle we're putting together!

Every time I turn around, you're off in a different direction somewhere. I get confused. I'm following you. *You're leading Me,* believe it or not!

Wherever you go, there I am, but you need to go first. When I see where you're heading, then I can make a way for you. But when you keep zigging and zagging and going backward on yourself, I just don't know what to do! It gets really confusing then. And I'm sure you're really confused too, because it seems I'm leading you one way, and then there's another opening going in a different direction, and then yet another and still another. You're wondering, *Which of these choices should I take?* And I'm saying to you, "Look at the choices you've already made."

The choices you've already made are directing the openings that are coming. *Those* choices are directing the paths that are opening. When you choose in *this* area then you choose in *that* area and then you choose in this area over here, and then you go in a different direction again, then there's another direction you try, and then something else calls to you, I don't know what you want!

Pick a path. Follow it. Stick with it for a while. Give Me an opportunity to follow up on your choices. Sometimes you make a choice to take you in one direction, and when something doesn't happen immediately upon making that choice, you decide you've made the wrong choice. But sometimes it takes time, time for Me to see what you've done and to put the pieces in place in the universe to make the next step happen for you.

Be patient once you make a choice and give me time to respond.

DAY 124: *You Came Here to Learn*

You came here to learn what it is like to be human, what it is like to struggle, to hurt. You came here to learn what it is like to be in love, to be happy and joyful, to be accepted, and yes, even to be rejected and abandoned and criticized! You came here to learn all these things. And you chose this lifetime, this path, to do it, because this is what you thought would be best at the time that we sat and talked together.

So instead of seeing yourself as a victim, recognize yourself as a co-creator. It will give you a much different perspective on what occurs in your life. It will help you, as you journey down the path, to accept it, to see it from a broader perspective, and it will help you see that there are other options. When you view things from a bigger perspective, there are more options available than when you view it through a narrow lens and only see one or two ways to go.

DAY 125: Listen to Your Heart's Voice

Listen to your heart's voice and follow it; *more often than not,* follow it! Begin, one step at a time, to put yourself at the top of your priority list. The more often you take care of you, the more often I can fill you up and give you what you need so you can give to and take care of the others around you.

You cannot pour a cup of tea from an empty pot, nor can you give from your heart if it is empty and depleted. And if it is empty and depleted and you are still trying to give, you will become frustrated and angry and resentful. And so *those* vibrations will taint anything and everything you are doing for those around you.

Treat yourself well first, from a place of loving yourself, and then take care of the needs of the others in your life.

DAY 126: I Work in the Silence

It is often in the deepest silence that I do My best work, without noise or fanfare, drums or whistles, without yelling or screaming or crying or gnashing of teeth. When you are simply sitting quietly, peaceful and at rest, tuned into Me or not, it makes no difference; it is the stillness I appreciate. Your life is often so frenetic, moving from one place to the next, a trillion, gazillion thoughts running through your mind, non-stop.

So when I have a moment, an opportunity to work in the silence of your being, I appreciate that moment. I accept it as a *gift,* and I use it to offer you *My* gifts.

DAY 127: Trust the Divine Voice

I need you. I need you to recognize the guidance. I need you to follow the guidance. I need you to let Me know what's working for you and what isn't. I need you to share with others that *we* are working together.

The only way this world is going to change is if everyone starts doing what you're doing: listening to the guidance, following that Divine voice instead of that snarky little voice inside of you that keeps telling you you're too small, you're not worthy, you're too fat, you're too short, you're too tall, you're not strong enough or good enough.

When you start listening to that Divine loving voice, you quell the snarkiness. You quiet the doubts. You increase your strength and your courage and your ability to manifest. I understand your fear. I understand you may doubt. It's part of your journey, your humanness. It's part of what you are learning: to put aside the human fears and trust in the Divine. It's why you're here.

DAY 128: *Change Your Exposure*

Acknowledge your uniqueness. Own it, recognize it, appreciate it, embrace it. Do not let anyone tell you that you are less than. And if there are those among your friends, your family, who treat you as less than, who speak to you as less than, then you have the ability to choose how much of that you wish to listen to, how much of that you wish to take in.

Perhaps it is time to limit your exposure to that which pulls you down and increase your exposure to that which builds you up. Your choice. Only *your* choice.

DAY 129: *Take Responsibility*

Watch your language when you talk about others in your life. How do you refer to them? In good terms or in terms that have judgment associated?

Remember that each time you speak a word that is associated with criticism or judgment, that is the vibration you are sending out. Sending out that vibration attracts that vibration to you and lowers whatever vibration you already were vibrating at because you chose to use those terms.

I'm asking you, from today forward, to think carefully about your words. Think carefully about your actions. Think carefully about your choices. Choose to speak differently. Choose to think differently. Choose to act differently, from a perspective of a higher vibration. Not as in right or wrong, but higher, for there are no wrongs. There are only choices, each choice carrying its own unique vibration. And don't tell Me, *don't tell Me*, and don't try and convince yourself, that you do not know which are the higher vibration choices, because you do.

Speak your truth to yourself first, then put that truth out to those who are with you, to those who love you, to those you come in contact with. Choose the higher choice. At least *most often*, choose the higher choice. And when you do choose the lower choice, choose it and take responsibility for choosing it. In that way, by choosing to accept responsibility for the choices you make and the actions you take, you actually raise that lower vibration to a higher place because you took responsibility.

DAY 130: *Call on Those in Spirit*

When you feel you are less than, when you feel you're drained or burned out or empty because of all that is taking place around you, it is important for you to remember to go within and ask for assistance, for we are here waiting, all of us!

I and all your guides and angels are here to assist you. All of those who love you and are already in the spirit world are also here, and capable of helping you in much greater ways than they could have helped you when they were in their human form. In their human form, like you, they got caught up in their old stuff, their woundedness, their pain.

So even when they were trying their very best in human form to do the very best for you, often their best looked sucky, because they were coming from their hurt rather than their hearts. But in spirit? They are beyond the humanness, and they can help you in greater ways than you can imagine.

DAY 131: *Be the Brightest Light*

The journey starts within you, in your heart. Heal yourself. Love yourself. Honor yourself. As your vibration goes higher and higher because of that love, you'll have so much more love to give. There will be so many more you can help—and not even by *doing* things for them, but simply by being who you are and letting them see how much happier you are, how much your self-confidence and self-worth have increased, how much brighter a light you shine wherever you go. You'll be the brightest light possible.

Think about what this world would look like if all of you were shining at your highest voltage, your brightest light. There would be no darkness anywhere!

So start inside of you. Start now. Tell yourself now how much you love yourself, how special you are, how amazing you are, what beautiful and unique and abundant gifts you have. Speak to your heart. Speak *from* your heart. Embrace the words. Embrace yourself.

DAY 132: Be the Co-Creator of Your Destiny

There are no accidents in this lifetime, no coincidences. There are only synchronicities. There is a reason for every single thing that occurs. You may not know the reason. You may not understand it. When you are nothing but spirit again, it will all be laid out in front of you, that bigger picture I talk about, that broader perspective.

Then you will see the plan. Not *My* plan for you, but *your* plan for you. And when you see that plan and how it's all unfolded? There will be a party. You will laugh as you have never laughed before because all of the pieces will finally fit together, perfectly in sync. And all of those who traveled with you in this lifetime, those who brought you joy and those who caused you pain and consternation? You will see how you all came together to do the work. You will see that you all *agreed* to do it. There were no victims. There were no perpetrators. There were only co-creators.

That's what you are, each and every one of you: a co-creator of your destiny. That's a lot of power that you have. How are you going to use it? What will you do with it? How will you help yourself and how will you help others? How will you serve? What can you give? What will you offer?

You are a powerful, powerful being. I could not have made you any other way. So I'm asking you to step up, to step out, to acknowledge your gifts, to embrace them, to own them, and to share them. I need you. This world needs you.

DAY 133: Focus on You

This is an important time. Embrace it. Relax into the support you have, into the love that is all around you. Allow yourself to be carried and supported. That is what you need right now to do the work you've come here to do.

You cannot give when you are empty. So fill yourself up, in whatever way calls to you: walking barefoot in the grass, digging in the dirt, walking on the beach, standing on a mountain and breathing that cool, fresh, crisp air, snuggling deep under the covers, shutting off your phone, closing your door—whatever it takes, whatever you need.

Right now, you are too empty to move forward, and anything you put your energy toward will drain you rather than enliven you.

You will know when you are ready. Don't rush the process. Allow yourself to gain the strength that you need, to rest, to feel good inside and out. You have been neglecting yourself for too long, trying to take care of others. It's time to focus on you and your needs.

DAY 134: Good Advice

Choose your words carefully. Let them come from your heart, not from your woundedness. Accept responsibility. Own your choices. Point your finger inward rather than outward.

DAY 135: You're Wasting Precious Energy

Holding on to the pain only keeps you stuck. It keeps you where you are so you are not free to take a step forward. Even when you attempt to take the step forward, one foot is behind you, stuck in the past.

Understand that each and every time you give energy to something that has happened in the past, something you can no longer change or effect by your thought or by the energy you give it, you are using up precious energy that you need in the *now* to help you heal, to help you be more of who you came here to be.

Perhaps, then, that is the reason you are holding on to the pain of the past. You are *afraid* of moving forward and have convinced yourself that the *past* is keeping you stuck so you *cannot* move forward. Actually, it is *you,* holding on to the past because you are fearful of what is to come. Your ego has convinced you that you need to stay where you are to heal.

I would say to you that to heal, you need to let go and move forward.

DAY 136: Ready Yourself

Many times you are uncertain where your path is leading you. You feel a yearning, an unrest, a call, but there is no definitive guidance as to what next step you are to take. You feel stuck, off balance, on the edge, not knowing where to put your next step and yet knowing that to put it in the usual place is not right, not what it used to be. You wait, off balance, uncertain, unsure. Sometimes the waiting is so long you begin to doubt there *is* a calling, thinking yourself crazy for believing what you are feeling could even remotely be true.

It is at these times especially that you most need to trust, to believe in yourself, in the Universe, in that Divine Source of All That Is. Trust you are right. Trust you are being called. Trust you are right where you are supposed to be. Trust . . . and wait.

Your time is coming, but *your* time is not *My* time. And while I work to put the pieces perfectly in place for your next step, rest. Ready yourself, love yourself, heal yourself, so when I call, when I finally call, you will be ready, perfectly ready, to answer and to follow.

Wait and trust and be okay with where you are, knowing that when *My time* is right, I will call and you will be ready to say yes. Trust.

DAY 137: *Open Doors Are a Call*

Honor your power. Embrace your light. Take the next step you are being guided to take.

There is no time but the present, no reason to wait, although you might convince yourself otherwise. There is an open door calling to you. There will be no punishment if you do not walk through the door, no negative consequences, just different consequences than if you choose to say yes and walk through the door now.

It will not be the only door that will ever open for you. There will, of course, be others. But right now you are primed for *this* door, for now, for this moment. It is up to you what you do with the opportunity. It is your choice to say yes or say no. I support the choices you make, whatever they may be. There are no negative repercussions. There never are. There are only responses to stimuli.

DAY 138: *Let Your Emotions Empower You*

It is not enough to speak your truth. For speaking your truth to have value, you must take action. Even a small step in a direction different from that which you have been going will work miracles to help get you unstuck and help you determine the true direction you should be walking.

You must walk your truth, not just speak it. You must walk through the fear. In fact, let the fear *companion* you on the journey. It is a powerful, *powerful* emotion that can help you move forward in ways you cannot even begin to imagine. *Harness* the power of that fear. Don't let it work against you. Allow it to work *for* you.

The same can be true of your anger and all the other negative emotions you may have buried within you. Free them so the power of those emotions can drive you forward, propel you forward, *shoot* you forward. Those things that you have been taught are negative are only different vibrations of energy. See them that way.

There is no positive or negative. What is, is. It is how you *use* those emotions that is positive or negative. Take those negative emotions, as you have called them for so long, neutralize them by getting rid of the word "negative" and allow them to propel you forward. *Use those emotions for your good.* There is so much *power* within them.

DAY 139: Go Within and Take Action

You have to put all the pieces in place *within you* so when all of the exterior pieces have been put in place, you are ready, you are ready to take that step. And there is nothing that will prepare you better than going within.

Now, spending time going within doesn't mean you don't take any action. Going within *is* an action. But if you go within to the point where you are not taking any *physical* actions of any kind to move forward, then you are using going inward as a way of not taking the steps forward! You are convincing yourself, rationalizing to yourself, that you are really doing the work, when, in fact, you have now turned going inward into a way of denying moving forward!

You have to go inward *and* you have to take action! It doesn't have to be big, dramatic steps, especially if you're not quite sure where you're supposed to go. You can do some research. If you feel like you're heading in one direction and you know there's information you're going to need—well, do some research. Find that information or at least make an effort to find it. That's one small step that will prepare you for the journey.

Sometimes, when you do that research, you end up finding other information that is, in fact, a guidepost to tell you what next step to take. There is always *something* you can do physically, some physical act of moving forward, while you are going inward. Both of those things are important and beneficial.

DAY 140: *Be Your Best Self*

I need you to be more. I need it for *you*, for your own growth and healing, *and* I need it for the world's growth and healing and expansion and change. As you shift your vibration and you move higher, you assist everyone who comes into your energy field in moving higher also. There's nothing conscious that you have to do except be the best you came here to be.

As you continue to work on yourself to heal more deeply, to understand and acknowledge and embrace your gifts, you will help all who come into contact with you to do the same. You give them an opportunity to be more. You have no choice in what they do with that opportunity. It is not in your control. All you have control over is who you are and what you do to help yourself move higher, to be your own best self.

DAY 141: Trust Your Core

Remember this: No matter who the messenger is, if the message doesn't resonate with you in the deepest core of your being, trust *your* core, *your* knowing. Go in the way that *your core* and *your knowing* and the Me that is *Me*—the great I Am Presence within you—is directing you!

DAY 142: You Amaze Me

I love you, you know. I truly love you. What beautiful hearts you all have! I really couldn't ask for more than what I have in each of you.

I wish you could love *yourself* as much as *I* love you. I wish you could know your *own* greatness as much as *I* know your greatness! I know you are a work in progress and you *are* getting better. My goodness, when I look back? Whew! Oh, my goodness! So much work you needed to do! But look how far you've come!

I know the journey hasn't been easy. For some of you, it's seemed interminable. For some of you, you've wished you could *end* the journey because it's been so painful and it was the only way out that you knew. And yet, you persevered. Somewhere deep down inside of you, you found the strength and courage you needed to continue, one small step at a time, to move forward. Sometimes I am truly amazed by your perseverance. Sometimes I wonder . . . If I were you, would *I* have the strength you have shown?

You are all such amazing, amazing, *amazing* gifts to Me! It is through each and every one of you that I know the fullness of My own being. I am grateful for the opportunity you each have given Me to share in experiences that I, otherwise, would not have if it were not for you and the courageous journeys each of you are taking.

DAY 143: *Use the Gifts I Give You*

I have given you *everything* you need. I have withheld from you that which would not serve you and bestowed upon you wondrous gifts—some of which are still buried within you because you are not quite ready to have them brought into being, into knowing. But they're there just waiting for you! When the time is right, if you allow them to, they will show themselves to you.

But understand when they come, I expect you to use them! I didn't give them to you just to let them sit in a drawer somewhere. I expect you to use them for your good, for *My* good, for all of those who will come to you because you have opened yourself up to Me. There is something I need you to do for each of *them* that they can only understand and accept from you.

Those who are in your circle of friends and relatives, those who pass by you on a daily basis, are all vibrating in a way similar to you, and they resonate with your vibration. Because of this, they can identify with you. They can look at you and say, "If she could do it, so can I!" or "If he can do it, perhaps he has the answers *I* need so *I* can do it, too."

But if you hide your gifts, how will they know? How will they find you? How will they know who to turn to in their darkest nights if you do not allow your own light to shine in its true form?

Give to Me what you are ready to release. Accept from Me that which I am offering, and you are willing to receive. Know there is a balance between the two, the releasing and the receiving, that in the end, will serve you well.

DAY 144: We Are Grateful

We are in this together, you and I. You are not traveling alone. I and so many others are always with you, always around you, always available to assist.

We are grateful for your presence here. Grateful for your willingness to continue healing yourself at an ever deeper level. Grateful to know you want to be more, do more, heal more deeply so you can enjoy life more completely. It is an honor to be of service.

DAY 145: *Do Your Own Work*

Keep in mind that you must do your own work. All your assistants and I cannot do it for you. We can only support you as *you* do the work.

It is necessary for you to take whatever continuing steps you need to take to facilitate further and deeper healing than that which you have already done. The guidance will come to you. The wisdom will be there and you will know what you need to do. I really encourage you to act on what you hear.

DAY 146: *Go Forward Without Expectations*

I ask you to go forward without expectations. I go forward with *you* without expectations, accepting completely whatever choices you make along the way as the ones that are best for you at this point in your journey.

Whatever you do, wherever your choices lead you, know that you are loved and cared for and supported, and I am always with you.

DAY 147: *Give Yourself Permission*

I sense a longing in you, deep within your heart. You allow it to come into your awareness from time to time, but then you take stock of your circumstances—your surroundings, your responsibilities, the ought-tos and the have-tos, the shoulds and the musts—and you quell the longing. You convince yourself it isn't important or that now's not the right time, and that someday, someday, someday . . .

You know, however, that tomorrow never comes, for *you are always in today.* And when you think you are in tomorrow—well, it has become today. So which day *is* your day?

When will you give yourself permission to listen to your heart? To understand you are worthy, to know you came here to be all you are capable of being—not to hold yourself back or keep yourself small because of others around you?

DAY 148: *Put Yourself in a State of Giving*

What are you giving back? To whom are you giving back? Or are your hands clutched tightly closed because you feel like you don't have enough, because there isn't anything coming in you can really depend on? So instead of giving, you are holding tight.

Well, can you understand that when your fists are tightly

clenched, it is true that nothing leaves, but also nothing comes in? If you want to receive, you have to give.

I'm not saying you should give in order to receive. I am only saying that when you *do* give, you will *always* receive. Not always in kind, of course. Just because you give $20 doesn't mean you'll get your return in money. You may get your return in a compliment. You may get it in a smile from someone who's never smiled at you before, or a hug when you need it. But you *will* get back what you give, and you will get it back multiplied. It *always* happens that way!

The problem often is that when you give in one form, you expect to receive in that same form. In fact, sometimes you give in a form you want to receive back in! That is the reason you give what you give.

I will say to you, let that go. You need to give because you *want to give*. You need to give because it makes you feel good to give. You need to give because giving takes you higher. It makes you more. It helps you grow and expand in amazing ways.

So, give. Give of your time. Give of your money. Give a smile to a stranger, a gentle touch where normally you might not have touched. Return a hug with meaning and intention. When you say to someone, "I will pray for you," sit down and pray for them! Don't just mouth the words and have it sound good. Do what you say you are going to do!

Put yourself in a state of giving and see what happens. Giving and receiving, they go hand in hand.

DAY 149: Be Humble

You are afraid of your own power, My power *within* you, the power I give you to be all you came here to be! After all, you and I are One!

If I am God, if I am the Divine Source of All That Is, if I am the I Am Presence, *so are you!* When you *own* that—truly, truly own it—can you even begin to imagine the power each of you has? Not only to heal yourself but to heal everyone else? That is a lot to comprehend. Is it any wonder you would find a way to disbelieve, to shut Me out, to close yourself down?

I want you, I want you dearly, to be everything you came here to be. I want *you* to be all that *I am* and more! "Greater works than these can *you* do when you do them in My name." You've heard that said time and time again. It's true.

There is nothing that holds you back but yourself. But I ask this of you: When you do My work, when you own the power within you that comes from that Divine Source of All That Is, I want you to own it humbly, with humility. I want you to give credit where credit is due. Yes, you do need to take credit for your own doing and your own being, because I am using you in ways that are specific to you because of your gifts.

And that makes you special! But it doesn't make you the only one who is special. There are many, many who are My instruments and

My messengers, who speak My name and do it freely and easily. But some of them are doing it because of ego rather than a willingness to serve humbly.

So I am asking you, I am begging you, I am *entreating* you, to be humble. Be all that you are, but with humility and grace. So much more will be accomplished *through* you when you work from humility than from ego.

DAY 150: I Won't Set You Up to Fail

I've been waiting for you. For such a long time, I've been waiting for you, patiently waiting. Waiting for you to come closer, to show Me you want a deeper connection, a more personal, intimate connection. Sometimes you come closer, inch by inch, bit by bit, and just when you begin to feel Me in your life in a bigger way, you back off.

What are you afraid of? Why is it that you fear *your* power and *My* power working within you? What are you afraid of? What old messages have you heard about Me? What old beliefs do you hold? What is it that you think will happen if you and I begin to co-create together?

I will not ask anything of you without providing you with all the tools and resources you need to accomplish that which I ask of you.

So there really is nothing to fear. I would never leave you unprepared. That would be foolish of Me, to ask you to do something and then not give you everything you need to accomplish it. I would never set you up to fail. That is not the way I work.

DAY 151: Trust That Little Voice

We need to talk more often, you and I. You need to listen more. You need to trust that when I am speaking to you, it's really *Me* speaking to you. Often you get the message but don't trust yourself. You don't believe it. You tell yourself, *It can't really be possible.* And you turn your back and walk in a different direction. Meanwhile, if you could look behind you, there I am, kicking and screaming and trying to get your attention. "Hey! Hey! Hey! It's Me, *Me.*"

Trust that little voice. The more you listen to it, the louder and stronger it will become. You just need to take a chance, take a risk. I have important work for you to do. But you can only do it if you recognize and appreciate the gifts you have and the gift that you are. I see all of that in you. I want you to see it in you, too.

DAY 152: Realign Yourself with the Divine

Tune in. Touch base. *Realign* yourself with that Divine Source of energy. When you are feeling low or empty or tired or run down, when you feel like there is no one else who cares about you, turn your focus *inward* to that space in the center of your being, that heart space.

Own the *fullness* of all that is there! Own *your* fullness through your connection with that Divine Source!

DAY 153: See Everything as a Happening

See everything that happens to you just as a *happening*. Don't assign good or bad, just look at it as a happening. Here I am now; tomorrow I'll be somewhere else. This is what's happening now; tomorrow something else will be happening. It's just a *happening*, an experience.

You humans are all so good at labeling things good or bad, better or worse than, less than, more than, higher than, lower than. It's what gets you into trouble! If you could stop labeling and just start *being* and *experiencing,* I think you would be amazed at how much easier your journeys would be, how much more you would *learn,* how much more quickly you would traverse the difficult times, and how much more you would enjoy the highs! You ought to give it a try! Just see what happens when you do.

DAY 154: Ready When You Are

Are you ready yet, or are you still playing that waiting game? Are you finding reasons, logical, rational, relevant (you think) reasons, or are you making excuses?

How honest can you be with yourself? How honest are you *ready* to be? You've already heard Me say I am here for you, but I can only take you where you are willing to go. I can't force you. I can only support you.

I would think by now that fence you're sitting on would be awfully hard and uncomfortable. And yet? You keep sitting there. Perhaps you have some padding I'm unaware of. I am very, very patient. I know when you are ready you will take the step off the fence. I just want you to know that when you do, I will be there for you, and you and I will travel together.

DAY 155: Find the Blessing

It is important when you have an experience that *appears* to be negative, that you work to find the blessing, the goodness, that comes from that experience.

I have not brought a negative experience to you. You have *chosen* a *choice*, and the choice you have chosen has resulted in the experience that has come to you. You made the choice because you needed the experience and the blessing that was coming to you from that experience. So it is important that you look to *find* the blessing, the goodness.

If, because of your state of mind or your emotions, you are unable to see anything positive out of what you ordinarily would have called a totally negative experience, I ask you to offer up gratitude anyway for the experience *and* for the blessings you've received. Even if you cannot see them, trust they are there.

DAY 156: Your Ego's at Work

I am here. I'm always here, always with you, companioning you on the journey. Sometimes you're aware of Me and other times you're sure you're totally alone as you walk the path. But I assure you, I am always, *always* with you on the path.

That feeling of aloneness is your ego working to convince you there is no *Force* concerned with you, no *Source* watching over you and providing for you. Your ego is trying to convince you so you will not take the next step to be a bigger, more expansive you. It's trying to keep you small and safe, trying to keep you where you are.

When you notice yourself getting stuck, going down that rabbit hole of negative thoughts and feelings and emotions, remind yourself that it's just your ego. Pay attention to what you're thinking and feeling and *choose* to think and feel differently. If you make the choice to do so, it's possible to do so. You just have to be willing and make the effort.

I would not bring you into being and allow you to be alone. You are too precious, too special, too much a part of Me for Me ever to abandon or reject you or turn away.

I am *in love* with you, fully and completely, always. And I love you deeply, every part of your being, every cell of your body. There is not a part of you I do not love.

DAY 157: What Will You Choose?

Free will, freedom of choice, it's all up to you. What are you choosing from here on out as you go forward? What actions will you choose? Or will you choose inaction? Will you choose to dig in your heels rather than walk along the path?

Even teeny, tiny, baby steps are better than standing in the same place on the path you have always stood. Staying in the same place will move you nowhere. So even the tiniest steps forward— uncertain as they may be—will still cause you to move forward and will still allow Me to shift things in ways I cannot shift them when you are standing stock still.

DAY 158: Walk a Divine Walk

Remember, I hold no judgment about how you walk your path. I only *hold you* as you walk your path. Always you are supported and loved and cared for. Always you are given everything you need. Even in the times when it feels like you have *nothing* that you need, you have *everything* you need because the feelings you are experiencing are what you need to experience to take you to the next level.

When you walk with Spirit, you must walk without your rose-colored glasses. You must walk without expectation, without desire. You must walk only with the intention of walking a *Divine walk* in whatever way, to whatever place, that leads you.

DAY 159: Do You Want the Baseball Bat?

The answers are within you. You just need to listen, to be present, to speak less and sit in the silence more. When you are busy doing and talking, busy running from one place to another, it is much more difficult for you to hear that which I am trying to say to you—especially the important things, especially if those important things are difficult things for you to hear.

Sometimes I think you *intentionally* keep yourself so busy that you cannot hear so you can pretend not to know. But sooner or later you will understand. The knowingness will come to you.

Do you want to have it hit you right upside the head? Do you really want the baseball bat? The Louisville Slugger? Wouldn't you rather have a gentle knowingness that just percolates up from within, bit by bit, little by little? It's so much easier that way.

DAY 160: *Let Me Help*

So many of you close your heart because you don't want to be hurt without realizing that when you close your heart to avoid being hurt, you've *closed in* the hurt that has already taken place, so it's trapped within you. There is no way for it to escape. And there is no way for healing to come in because there is no entrance, just as there is no exit. You are afraid that if you open up now, after all this time, that it will hurt tremendously. And yet I would say to you, the hurt will be worse if you continue to stay closed off.

It is a matter of choice . . . your choice. I will support whatever choice you make, so tell Me what you want. Tell Me how you want it to be. Take action to make it so and I will support those actions. But don't tell Me you want it to be a particular way and expect *Me* to be the one who does it all. It doesn't work that way. *I* don't work that way. I follow *your* lead.

Show Me what you want, where you want to go. Begin to move in that direction and I will move Heaven and Earth to make it happen for you. The journey you were so afraid of, that you thought would be so long and hard and miserable, will be covered in a much shorter period of time and with much less difficulty than you could even begin to imagine.

You don't have to do it all yourself, but that's what you are trying to do. Let Me help you. Talk to Me. Work with Me. Together we can make the changes happen. Let Me help. Let Me help you find your wholeness, your completeness, your beingness. Just let Me help.

DAY 161: I Hold Us Both Accountable

I love you all so much. There is *nothing* I would not give to make *your* journey, *every* journey, an easy one, to see you laughing and joyful and blissful, *rapturous* even!

But you? As spirit, you have chosen other paths because there were lessons to be learned from those experiences that were less than that. You have asked Me to accompany you on the journey and to keep you on track, to hold you to that which you told Me you wanted to learn before you were born—an agreement I promised I would keep for you, even when, in your humanness, you wished it to be otherwise. I love you enough to do this for you, even when it hurts Me to see what My loving you this much is doing.

If I did not love you so much, I could not hold Myself accountable to that which you've asked of Me. Even though I love you *this much*, it is still difficult to do when I see that what you have asked of Me causes you pain or suffering, causes you to be wounded or in doubt, causes you to feel unworthy or unloved or guilty. But I am strong enough to hold us both accountable, and so I will, because you have asked Me to.

I am probably the only one in your life who has never broken a promise to you. Even though I am, most likely, the one who has made the *biggest* promises and the ones that are most difficult to keep because they require Me to stand aside as I *watch you grow* . . . through your fear, through your pain, through your doubt. Those are difficult promises to keep.

But because I love you so very much, so deeply, to the very core of *our* being, I allow Myself to experience the suffering *with* you so you might grow and become all you have chosen to become on this journey now.

DAY 162: *Your Hands Are the Only Hands I Have*

We work together, you and I. We co-create. Do you understand that your hands are the only hands I have, and without your hands, there is nothing I can do? Without the love in *your* heart, how can *I* show love? I need you as instruments, as messengers, as emissaries. I need you each to be the best you can be to do the work you came here to do. Each of you has a place. Each of you has a purpose. Each of you has talents and gifts and skills and abilities that are unique unto you.

Think about how many painters there are in the world, how many painters there have been throughout history . . . and no two painters paint alike! Think about composers and how each composition differs from every other. Think about all the mothers in the world and how each one parents differently and uniquely.

Each of you is needed! It doesn't matter if there are fifty thousand who are doing what you are doing. Every one of the fifty thousand is unique and different and has its own unique vibration. And there is nothing about you that is less than. There is nothing about you that is not qualified to do whatever it is you are being called to do. There is not one of you who doesn't have every single thing you need to do what you are being called to do, unless you choose to believe it is so.

Sometimes I just want to shake you to help you see how beautiful you are, how smart you are, how loving, how kind, how gentle a heart you have! I wish I could reach out and shake you and wake you up, open your eyes to see yourself as I see you: so beautiful, so perfect, each and every one of you! Each of you a child of the Divine. Each of you perfect, exactly as you are. Even those things you identify as warts or imperfections, there is nothing imperfect about them. They are perfectly suited to the journey, to this life you have chosen. They make you who you are and what you are. They help you be who you came here to be. They help you do what you came here to do, to learn the lessons you came here to learn.

The next time you look in the mirror and you're tempted to berate yourself, to call yourself less than, I want you to hear My words. I want you to see yourself as I see you: perfect in every way, perfectly suited for the work that is yet to be done, perfectly suited for the path you are walking and the path that will open up as you continue to move forward.

DAY 163: Untangle Your Feelings

Tangled and twisted, so many feelings tangled and twisted; feelings from the past, feelings from the present, worries about the future. Everything tangled and twisted. Nothing seems clear.

You gaze at one path and for a moment, think, *This is the way!* Then something else comes along and you say, "No, this is the way!" And then you think back, you feel, you *feel* the connections to the past, and you think, *No, I can't go any of those ways. I have to do this!* You make your choices from a place of have to, and ought to, and this is what is expected, rather than this is what you want and desire, what your heart needs.

It's time to unwind, to untwist, to separate the strands of the past, the present, and the future and focus on *this* moment. In each and every moment, focus here, *in the now.* Make the best choice you can, looking at what it is in *this* moment you can do if you're willing and ready.

Allow the knots to unknot. Allow the threads to untwist. Allow yourself to be aware of what your heart is saying *to* you, *about* you and *for* you. Put your focus on your heart space and trust that what you hear is exactly what you need to hear to enable you, to empower you, and yes, to embolden you!

DAY 164: *Be Grateful for the Evidence of Healing*

Give gratitude, always, for that which you are going through. Let Spirit know you understand that these uncomfortable symptoms are just a measure of all that you were that no longer fits and is being released. Let Spirit know you are grateful for the work that is being done . . . so grateful!

How many times have you heard that "thank you" is the only prayer you need to utter? Sometimes, when you are in the throes of the deepest release, even saying "thank you" seems to be beyond your ability to do.

But just whisper it. Just think it. Just be in gratitude and allow the process to be everything you need it to be to move you higher.

DAY 165: *Appreciate the Bumps*

No matter how bumpy the journey once you begin, the bumps are *teaching* you something. Don't be afraid to learn!

You're so quick, each time something "negative" happens, to judge it as negative, to label it as bad, to say it is a mistake. Why not, instead, look at it with wonder and amazement and say, "Hmmm . . . What has this come to teach me? How blessed I am to have this bump in my road, this chasm outside my door, this gorge that doesn't appear to have a bridge across it! How blessed I am to be given the opportunity to learn a new way: a different way, a bigger way, a more powerful way, a more trusting way!"

Very rarely do I hear you thank Me for those bumps! More

often, you *curse* the bumps, and in cursing the bumps, curse Me as well. Yet, I have put no bump before you that you have not asked Me to put in place so you could learn what you came here to learn.

My message to you is always the same: You and I, we sat and *co-created* all of these experiences before you came here. You told Me this is what you wanted, so I am helping you accomplish it. Yes, sometimes you have to be uncomfortable to learn the lesson, but often the *biggest* blessings come when you are the *most* uncomfortable, the most uncertain, the most fearful of the steps you are planning to take and you take them anyway.

DAY 166: Stretch Yourself

Stretch yourself! Stretch yourself *beyond* your comfort zone, beyond your known limits. Stretch! Reach up high, as if you could touch the very top of the sky where it meets the heavens! And if you fall a little short in your estimation, remember that I have no such thoughts of your failure. Every single attempt you make, every step you take, is the perfect step in *My* estimation of you.

So whenever you take a step, I am pleased! I am as proud of you as a first-time parent who watches his child take that very first step alone and unaided, wobbly, uncertain, and yet, a face filled with joy at the accomplishment! That is Me when you take that step.

Just as an infant takes steps between birth and that first step to be able to *make* that first step, you also have to take steps, baby steps, then bigger steps, and bigger steps. Eventually, yes, you might take a leap of faith! Maybe you'll just stumble into faith! It doesn't matter how you get there. And it doesn't matter how far you think you are along the journey, or how far you still have to go.

What matters? What matters is that you keep putting one foot in front of the other, time and time and time again. That's what matters.

DAY 167: *Be the Instrument*

Say yes and be willing to be the instrument! You know all about instruments. They are played. They vibrate. They stir up emotions. They bring up thoughts and feelings that you've kept buried.

Instruments are very, very, very powerful. So if instruments are powerful and you are an instrument, then you, too, are powerful in ways you cannot even begin to understand. Nor should you. Because if you tried to understand how it all worked, you'd keep yourself too busy thinking about the hows and the wheres and the whys to be a clear and open channel, to *be* that perfect instrument. It's like when you strike a chord on the piano. If the strings are uncluttered, unfettered, if there is a clear pathway, the tone is clear and true. But if something falls upon the strings and blocks the vibration, the sound is not quite as pretty, not as easy to listen to.

I don't want your minds or your hearts to be cluttered with questions. I don't want you to try and figure out when it's going to happen or how. I just want you to be willing to be used, willing to serve as an instrument, as a channel, as a messenger, willing to be the hands I don't have, the body I don't have, except your own.

DAY 168: All Ways Are Equal

I ask you to avoid comparing yourself to any other. Stand firm in the knowledge and the knowing that I am working within you in exactly the right way for who you are at this stage in your journey.

There are some of you, have no doubt, that are ready to run and leap, even when the running and the leaping is without a definite destination. There are those of you who will tentatively put your toes into the water. There are others who will walk the path at just a medium rate, but unafraid as each step is lighted to take that step and plant both feet firmly upon it.

Each of these ways is equally appropriate, equally good, equally positive. Each is exactly what you need in the way you need it most to allow you to open up to that which is within you in a way that does not frighten you, that does not scare you away, that does not overwhelm you.

DAY 169: We Experience Time Differently

Some of you are slow learners. Some of you are pretty quick! And some of you are slow at one time and quick at another.

It always amazes Me what takes you so long to learn and what you pick up so quickly! I can never figure it out! Sometimes I'm in such a quandary when I'm working with you. Why can't you just *get it?* It's not a judgment. I don't get it! *I just don't get it!*

But My time and your time, they're two different times. That's for sure! Blink of an eye? Hmmm . . . Sometimes that's what it seems like for Me, but for you? Oh, my gosh, it's years and years and *years* stuck in the same place. We see differently, you and I, but we are here working together on everything.

DAY 170: But for the Grace of Choice

I love you each. I love you each uniquely, separately, different-ly because each of you is unique—and yet, ultimately, each of you is the same because you each carry My Divine Spark in your heart space. So each of you is *of* Me, which makes each of you *of* one another, and of *all* others.

It is when each of you, and everyone, stops seeing themselves as separate that there will be peace. Remember as you go forward today that the Spark that is in your heart is the Spark in every other person's heart also. When you do something out of character to that Spark—when you do something from a place of fear or anger, when you see yourself as separate—rather than raising the vibration of the world, you lower your own vibration and the vibration of all who are around you.

You cannot see yourself as better than, for "there but for the Grace of God", you might be in the other's shoes. Reach out gently. *Reach out*, always with the intent that from you comes the highest of all vibrations. In even the most difficult times, in the most difficult ways, to the most difficult person, send out vibrations of unconditional love, remembering it is not *your* unconditional love you are sending, it is *Mine*. Send My unconditional love from your heart to theirs, and I will heal *your* heart in a deeper way so that eventually you also feel that unconditional love.

DAY 171: *Reach Out in Peace and Love*

Daily there are instances when you can reach out in peace and love. Become aware of them. Alert yourself to the possibility that you are being called upon to help. Know that within you lies the power to be of assistance to all around you—not only in ways that are outwardly recognizable but in ways that are quiet and subtle and may go completely unnoticed.

There is great power even in the smallest of events in which you reach out to help another, be they human, animal, plant, insect. One never knows the full repercussions or implications of one's actions. One never knows how far-reaching the gentlest touch, the simple smile. One never knows. But trust that each gesture, each kindness, each touch of healing hands will benefit not only those who are before you but many others in ways you cannot even imagine.

DAY 172: *Be in Alignment*

When you find yourself caught in the emotions of a situation, when you hear the words coming out of your mouth and feel the emotional energy of those words, allow yourself the opportunity to consider if the energy of your words is in alignment with the goal, the objective you are reaching for.

If you find there is a misalignment, if you find there is not a match, it is a sign that you have work to do, that you need to excavate the foundation of those emotions and discover the origin. You need to understand yourself in a bigger way, a deeper way, so as you move forward, as you are touching more and more lives, as you are acting as a guide, a mentor, a teacher and a model for all who come to you, you are, more often than not, in complete and total alignment on all levels.

DAY 173: Live a Balanced Life

Trust in Me more deeply. Sit with Me and give Me time, but make time for yourself and for the pleasures in your own life also. Expand yourself in ways you haven't before because you were too afraid, too panicked, too anxious, too busy. Step out in ways that make you laugh and giggle. Step out and be playful, not just serious and spiritual. A *balanced* life is what you need.

You have been focused for so long on the difficult areas of your life that you truly have not experienced all the joy that is possible for you to experience. So push yourself to new limits in *those* areas, those areas of playfulness and fun. Give yourself some time to laugh and love, to relax, to be totally at peace with who you are and where you are.

DAY 174: *You Are Greatly Blessed*

You have been greatly blessed, each of you.

Yes, sometimes the blessings are couched in pain and suffering, loss and woundedness. Your job is to peel back the layers of what appear to be the negatives so you can find the positives, so you can find the blessings and opportunities and gifts that are present in all of what you call the *challenges* in your life. You know that saying: "From the biggest risks come the greatest rewards." You just need to be able to recognize them!

And sometimes you just have to trust that they're there even when you cannot see them, because sometimes in this lifetime, you are really not meant to *see*. You are simply meant to *trust*.

DAY 175: *Step into Your Greatness*

I love you, you know, each and every one of you, with all your fallibilities, all your imperfections, all your issues. I don't see any of those things as making you less than in My eyes. They are just the challenges you came into this life to conquer, to carry, to work through and around. They are just a part of who you are. *They don't make you less than!* Although in your own eyes, you often see yourself as less than because of them.

You are powerful creatures, each and every one of you. I am going to encourage you, challenge you, to step out of your comfort zone and into your power zone. Now, I won't berate you if you stay in the comfort zone. I won't love you any less, and I will *support you* with either choice you make.

If I'm going to support you in the comfort zone *and* support you in the power zone, why would you *not* take the step into the power zone? Why would you not step up and be *all* you are capable of being? Because you *will* be given all you need. You will be shown that all you need is *within* you because *I* am within you. You forget that the Divine Source of All That Is resides *within you*, in your heart space. That is where I am.

Let go of your need to be safe and comfortable. Let go of your fears and your worries and your anxieties and your tensions. Let go of feeling less than and step into your greatness! Step into it and own it and see what happens!

DAY 176: *Embrace Who You Are*

If you are ready and willing, I can take it all from you; but you need to be willing and ready to accept whatever changes will come as a result of releasing it, of letting it go. You have to make changes in your behavior, find new ways of being. You have to let go of old ways that are no longer serving you. Let go of old expectations, old messages you've received, old thoughts of not being good enough, not being smart enough, not being whatever it is you have that message in your head about. Let all that old stuff go. Recognize you have every single thing you need within you and it becomes empowered and enlivened when you let go of all those old things!

But unless you let go of the old ways, the old beliefs, the old messages, there is no room for the new. There is no room for that new belief that is really the original knowing that you are plenty good enough, that you are completely, perfectly good enough.

You have to get rid of the old so you can embrace being who you *really* are.

DAY 177: Branch Out

It's time for you to branch out, to try *new* things! Sometimes you become too familiar with that which is comfortable and you fail to look outside that box you have been so comfortable in.

There are other things out there that can help take you higher, help make you bigger, help you expand. Seek them out and *test* them out! Open yourself to the possibilities that will present themselves to you and do so with joy and openness!

DAY 178: Keep Me Front and Center

Don't forget Me. Keep Me front and center always, especially in your darkest moments when there is no one else you can rely on, no one you feel safe to call upon. Call *My name*. Bring *Me* in. I am always with you but I can only intercede when you invite Me. Unless you ask for My help, I must stand beside you and watch as you try and do it all alone, or as you seek help and assistance from others who are less capable and less willing and less loving than I am. So ask *Me*.

And I care not what name you call Me. Don't get caught up in names. There is no right name, no wrong name. *Assign* Me a name if it will help you get closer to Me. I will take no offense by whatever name you designate for Me. I will simply be grateful you have chosen, at long last, to come closer, because at that point we will have been apart much, much too long.

DAY 179: You Came Here to Be More

You all came here for a reason. You all chose this life and these experiences to help your soul learn the lessons it needs to learn, and it came here to be *more*, not less!

Now, being more doesn't necessarily mean you stand on a stage and speak before millions. Being more can simply mean you are the very, very best at *whatever it is* you're doing—whether that's digging a ditch, caring for those who need to be cared for, speaking from a podium, scrubbing toilets, styling someone's hair, or helping to serve the masses. Not everybody is supposed to be in the spotlight, but you *did* come here to be your best self!

And with every choice you make, whether it's the higher vibration choice or the lower vibration choice, you *are* being your best self.

DAY 180: *Make Higher Vibration Choices*

With each and every choice you make, choose the choice that opens you up more. Choose the choice that says yes instead of no. Choose the choice that brings you closer to Me instead of pushing Me away. Choose that higher vibration choice. As you do, you will continue to see more and more doors open, and more and more blessings and gifts and abundance come your way.

That's not to say there won't be times of difficulty and challenge, for there will! That's part of your human journey. But what it does mean is that each and every time there seems to be a glitch, a hole, a bump in the road, you will have everything you need to get through it. You will come through it more easily than you ever thought possible, more easily than you used to because now you have more tools. You have more trust. You have more faith. You know that you are not alone. You know that everything you need will be provided and more.

DAY 181: Hold the Bigger Picture

I suggest that you teach yourself to hold the bigger picture. Even when you cannot *see* the bigger picture, *trust* there *is* one. Perhaps there is even a reason you are not being shown it. Perhaps the bigger picture would scare you half to death because you would see where you are going and you are not ready, not because it is a *bad* place to be, but because it is an *amazing* place to be and you don't yet know that you have the ability to do what you will need to do once you get there. You can't imagine you are so *amazing* that you'll be able to do those things! You can't imagine you are so fantastic and so gifted! So intelligent! So talented!

It's so much easier to think you *can't* do it, because then, of course, if you believe you can't, so much less is expected of you. *You* expect so much less of yourself! You settle into the "can't do" instead of the "can do" and allow yourself to relax a bit because you think you can't do it anyway. So you think *Why try?* . . . not understanding that if you just take the step to do it, you will! And if you don't end up *exactly* where you thought you wanted to, you'll find that where you end up is exactly where you were *supposed* to end up anyway! You just got there in a different way. You had to let go of your expectations. You had to let go of the reins. You had to step out of needing to control and just surrender.

DAY 182: *All Choices Lead to Learning*

No choice that you make is wrong because all choices lead to learning. So whatever choice you make at every moment, at every juncture in your life, you are making because what comes after the choice is exactly what you need to learn to take you to the next step, even if the lesson that comes to you is one that seems as if you would never have chosen it for yourself.

DAY 183: Trust and Faith Are Important

I am here for you always, even when you cannot see Me or feel Me or hear Me. Even if you believe you do not know Me, I am here for you always.

There will not always be a physical manifestation of My presence in your life. There will not always be a perfect knowing of Me in the times when you most need to know Me. It is about your trust in Me and your faith that the promises I have made to you, I keep.

If others in your life have made promises and broken them, you need to know I am not like them. Everything I have promised you has always, always, *always* been given to you.

It is often necessary, however, to give you what you ask for in ways that are not the ways you've asked to receive it. Sometimes what you've asked of Me is not what you most needed . . . and I, I give you what you *most* need at the time you ask.

So trust and faith are important factors as you move forward into the unknown, as you take this next step on your journey, as you separate from what was, and move into what is, and go forward into what you are becoming.

DAY 184: *Begin to Listen*

If you want a deeper channel, a greater connection, if you want to feel Me more powerfully in your life and have Me guide you more deftly through the channels, begin to listen to what I am saying to you in that small, quiet voice in your head about how to love yourself better.

And then you will hear more about other aspects of your life, and even, perhaps, about the aspects of others' lives, if that is what you desire to know. But for your sake, listen to the guidance about your *own* self.

Listen! Follow! Pay attention! Do!

DAY 185: How You Travel Makes the Difference

Sometimes you can be your safest in the most uncomfortable of situations if you are uncomfortable because you have stepped outside your comfort zone and put yourself in a new and bigger zone, the next zone up. Safer because you are saying to Me, "I trust You to care for me as I take this higher step. I trust that as I listen to my heart and make the choices that fulfill my heart's desire, You are with me every step of the way."

Even when you are on a roller coaster ride in life, going up and down, that seems to have no end, I am with you! I have you locked tightly into the seat. Just as in a physical roller coaster the bar is across your lap holding you in, *I* am the bar that holds you safe on this roller coaster you call life!

There is no easy road. There is no difficult road. *There is just a road!* How you *travel* it is what makes it difficult or easy. How you accept or not where you are makes it difficult or easy. How you view what happens to you makes it difficult or easy.

DAY 186: *Move into Your Power Zone*

I want you all in your *power zone*, not your comfort zone! In your comfort zone, you forget that you are empowered! In your comfort zone, you are content to be who you are, to be the small person your comfort zone can hold. Whereas I, I wish for you to be the biggest, largest expansion of energy you can possibly be and your comfort zone can't hold that!

You don't have to tear down all the walls at the same time. You can simply open a window or a door. Crack them if that's all that feels safe, but at least *open up* the comfort zone!

Feel that breath of fresh, empowering air and energy and love that comes when you have the courage to open the door, crack the window, tear down the walls and step out. When you think of doing it, though, what you think of is *I'm so scared!*

I'm encouraging you, *challenging* you, to say instead, "I'm so damned excited! I can't wait to do this!" Okay, so maybe there'll be a little scaredness underneath the "I'm so damned excited!" But use the energy of the fear to empower the excitement and *push you through that door!*

DAY 187: *Become Reacquainted with Your Spirit*

This is a time for seeking out, for searching, for getting to know. This is a time for stepping outside the limits of that which you know, and allowing yourself to experience that which you long for but which is still a mystery to you.

How can you long for something you do not know? It is only your humanness that is ignorant. Your spirit knows all. So let your physical self, your humanness, and your spirit connect in a deeper way. Tune into the inner knowing, the inner longing. Allow yourself to reacquaint yourself with your spirit. You have been separate far too long!

DAY 188: *Work to Develop Your Gifts*

I'm asking you to take a leap of faith, to trust Me in a deeper, greater way, perhaps in a more unique way than you've ever trusted before. I will honor your trust. I will not abuse it. And you will see yourself grow in ways you never even imagined.

Your path will open in ways that you have never contemplated before. It does not mean you will become a miracle worker. That's your ego speaking. It simply means that whatever work you have come here to do will manifest.

Some of you came to be the light under the bushel, that steady, stable, guiding light that everyone knows can always be depended on. You're not on stage. You're not in the spotlight. No one knows your name except for the small circle of people around you who depend on that steady, steady, steady light. For now, for this journey, for this lifetime, that is why you are here.

For others, you may be asked to take a step outside the norm for you, to step out of the box, step out of your comfort zone. Perhaps you will be asked to take the stage, to speak to many, to allow the gifts inherent in you to show themselves to others who may be skeptical, who may be judgmental, who may criticize. But in those groups where there are critical doubters, disbelievers, there will be seekers. There will be those for whom you are the teacher, the guide, the mentor, the opener of the door they have been seeking.

Whether you speak in a big, bold voice or a small, soft voice, those who are supposed to come to you will come to you as long as you *do* speak, as long as you allow them to know the gifts and talents you have worked to bring forth. And you must work. You must practice. You must set aside time to develop those gifts in whatever ways work for you. It needs to be a conscious effort if you wish to get it into the subconscious, because there needs to be a shift from one level of awareness to the other.

DAY 189: *Manage Your Energy Wisely*

Do you realize that all those energies you give to wondering about tomorrow and the next day and the next, all those energies are being *wasted* on those tomorrows? You can't direct them toward thoughts of tomorrow and have them available to work for you today.

Every time you think about a "what if" or "what will be", that is energy you have given to something you have no knowledge of and no control over, energy you have lost that could be put to use for what you are doing today.

So stay as present in the now as you can. Manage your resources wisely. Be all you can be in *this* moment, and I will take care of the next. That is all I am asking of you. Just be present in the moment.

DAY 190: *Allow Yourself to Receive*

The struggle is never ending because *growth* is never ending. Sometimes there will be times of peace, relatively, when things are all going smoothly. Everything seems easy. All of the pieces are in place. And there will be other times when you are on level four rapids and can't even find the paddle to help you steer where you need to steer.

But make no mistake, you *always* have what you need. You are always being steered and guided as long as you are *open* to being steered and guided. You *can* decide that you are strong enough to do it all yourself. It will make your struggle, your growth, your expansion and your journey more difficult because you are not open to receiving Divine help. Most often, when you are in that mode, you are not open to receiving *anyone's* help.

I am asking you to allow yourself to receive the help that is being offered, even from the most unlikely sources and at the most unlikely times. Say, "Yes!" Say, "Yes!" Say, "Yes!"

DAY 191: *Open Yourself to Divine Providence*

I'm not asking you to take a giant leap. I'm not asking you to scale the mountain or jump the gorge. I'm just asking you to take a step in the direction you're being called to go—one small, tiny step, one action in that direction.

Can you do that? Are you willing to do that? And then, after you take that step, take another, then another, then another and another. Eventually, they'll be bigger steps because you'll have the faith. You'll have the courage. You'll have everything you need, and what will happen is you'll see that I *will* give you all you need. The Universe will provide.

But you have to keep taking the steps. You can't take one or two then stop and say, "Okay, now you do it all, God." I don't work like that. I *support* the steps *you* take. When you stop taking steps, so do I. But when you keep taking steps one after the other after the other, and you build momentum? Oh my goodness, the vibration! The energy! The flow that comes, that happens! You get caught up in the flow and everything seems to go so much more smoothly. Pieces fall into place. Things happen in magical ways, in *unimaginable* ways. Your rational, logical mind could not ever have conceived of some of the things that will happen!

But when you're caught in the flow, life becomes more magical and mystical. And that rational, logical way that other people live? It's not your way of being anymore, because you're tapped in. You're plugged in. You're in the flow! Isn't that where you'd rather be? Isn't that how you'd like to live your life, plugged into that flow, each and every moment of each and every day?

That doesn't mean there won't be hard times, challenges or problems. What it *does* mean is that you won't be walking that path alone. You'll have help. You'll have amazing ways of figuring out what needs to be figured out. And sometimes things will get figured out without you doing the figuring! You'll be trying to figure out how they got figured out!

That's what happens when you're in the flow, when you trust, when you open yourself to Divine Providence. What an amazing way to live!

DAY 192: *Honor Your Emotions*

I'm not saying you shouldn't experience your emotions. Absolutely you should be delighted when it's a wonderful outcome or an even better outcome than you expected. And yes, it's okay to be sad or disappointed or angry or resentful, or whatever emotion comes up, when your choice ends up in a way other than you wanted it to.

You're human, so you have to honor those emotions; but you have a choice as to whether you wallow in them or honor them. Wallowing in them means you get stuck in them; they take you down the rabbit hole and you can't figure out the next step to take.

Honoring them means you experience them. You acknowledge them. You say, "Okay, this is what I'm feeling because of what happened." And then? And then you *decide* what you're going to *do* next, which is the exact same process that happens when it's an absolutely delightful outcome! You still have to decide what you're going to do next. The process is always the same whether you label the outcome good or bad. Now isn't that interesting?

Something for you to chew on. Something for you to think about the next time you make a choice and the outcome is something other than you wanted or expected. I hope you'll remember that we talked about this. It will be very helpful if you do.

DAY 193: *Create Miracles with Me*

What happens if you open yourself fully to the flow of life? Where will it take you? What does it mean if you are truly and completely in the flow? Is there something to fear by being in that flow? A loss of control? A lack of knowing?

I will not take you anywhere you are not ready to go. Nor will I take you anywhere and not give you the tools, the resources and the information you need to follow the path you're on. That would be foolish of Me.

So I am encouraging you to open yourself to all possibilities and know I have your back. Know that there is nothing you can try that I will not provide you with all you need to accomplish it. I just ask you to be willing to do so, to trust Me and have faith . . . and have faith in yourself.

You are a powerful instrument for good. Embrace *your* power. Open yourself to *My* power. *Together, we will create miracles.*

DAY 194: *How Should the Signs Appear?*

Watch for signs and messages. Ask for signs and messages that you are, indeed, on the right path. If an idea comes to you about a step you need to take, I have no problem if you ask Me to repeat a sign to let you know you are definitely going in the right direction. Just tell Me what sign you want to appear because I don't want you to miss the message should I give it to you in a form that you aren't expecting.

So many of you are so sure you're *not* receiving any messages. It isn't that you aren't receiving them, it's that you're not allowing yourself to recognize them for what they are. Perhaps it's because you want them in a different form or shape, or to come at a different time in a different way. I don't know. So tell Me! *Tell Me* what sign you need!

Do you need an orange butterfly to appear three times in a row? Do you need to see a hawk circling overhead? Do you need to see a turtle along the path or perhaps a fox in the meadow? Do you need your mother to say "I love you" when she's never spoken those words before?

Just tell Me what it is you need. Just tell Me what sign, what message will convince you that I am here and hearing you, and available to work with you. I wish only to draw you closer, to cement our connection. So whatever it takes, I will do.

DAY 195: *Every Decision Impacts the Outcome*

As long as you put all the pieces in place that you have control over or are aware of, the final outcome will be what it's meant to be.

No matter where you end up in this lifetime, it is where you are supposed to be! There are no accidents. There are no mistakes.

Your life is a journey of purpose and intention, whether you recognize it or not. Every choice you make helps lead you to the final outcome. Even your smallest decisions impact the outcome in some way. As you make your choices—what cup of tea to drink, whether or not to have that second piece of chocolate cake, or give up sugar, or stop using the microwave, whether to take another step outside your comfort zone in an even bigger way—each and every one of those choices is important in the grand scheme of things. Of course, some are more important than others, but all are still important.

If you are moving to a higher vibration, it's important that you continue to make more higher vibration choices. There will be times when you will make lower vibration choices. That is because it's what you need to be able to move forward; but the more often you can make the higher vibration choices, the less often you will be tempted to make the lower ones.

The choice is always yours, and I always support whatever choice you make.

DAY 196: Step Out in Faith

You long for peace, for safety, for certainty, for security. You want to know where you're going to end up *before* you take the first step; but faith doesn't work that way. You have to have faith when you take the first step that all you need will be provided, and you have to step out in that faith, even if you can't see the next step. You need to keep stepping out that way, one step at a time. As you do, and as you see how all of us support you, how the Universe supports you, it gives you more and more courage to take the next step, and the next and the next and the next.

And yes, it is true, as you continue to step out in faith and trust, I will ask you for a bigger faith, a deeper trust. I will ask you to do more and be more because I need you to be more. The *world* needs you to be more. The gifts you have within you are not yours to keep buried. They are yours to share, to use, to help yourself and to help others.

So I need you to step out in faith. I need you to plumb your depths and search for your gifts if you don't already know what they are. And if you have an idea? If you have an inkling? I need you to open yourself up to that inkling. I need you to explore that. Take it out, shine the light on it, and see if, "Yes, this is my gift. Or no, I was mistaken. There is something else I am meant to do."

You know what I'm talking about. You've been feeling the urge. You have felt that there is more you are being called to do.

Go within. See what gifts you have lying within you, waiting for you. Bring them out into the light so they can grow. Water them. Nourish them. Support them. Encourage them. Embrace them. Be aware of them.

You did not receive your gifts by accident. I gave them to you with a purpose in mind. Your job is to open yourself to your gifts and allow them to guide you.

As you give yourself permission to know yourself, I will give you all that you need to express yourself.

DAY 197: Know That I'm Holding the Space

Things have happened the way they have happened—especially those things you thought would happen in a different way, that you had an expectation of a different outcome—they've happened because you told Me what you were coming into this lifetime to learn. I agreed to it when you were in spirit.

We have a contract, you and I. You are holding Me accountable to the lessons you said you wanted to learn. Because of your free will, your free choice, and because I gave you that gift and won't take it back, I have to go by the choices you made when you were in spirit and said, "This is what I want to learn." You asked Me to be accountable and responsible to see that you learned them, and that's what I'm doing.

So for those of you who pray, for those of you who beseech and beg (because there are those of you who do that and think I do not hear your prayers, that I'm totally oblivious and that somehow you must have fallen through the cracks and I don't even know you exist), understand that I *am* answering your prayers. I'm answering your prayers by holding Myself accountable to the agreement we had.

Sometimes you may hate Me. Sometimes you may think I hate you, or at the very least, am ignoring you, but I am not. Trust Me when I tell you that when I see you suffering because of a choice you've made, I am suffering with you.

Can you imagine being a parent whose child is in trouble and wanting to help, but not being able to because you were told that you couldn't? That's Me. I'm here watching, supporting. I am here suffering as you suffer. I am here holding the space for you to learn that which you came here to learn, because at that moment in time, all you are permitting Me to do is hold the space.

DAY 198: You Have Influence

You are a force for good. You are a mechanism for change just by being who you are. Everyone who comes into your energy field as you continue to heal and raise your vibration, has an opportunity to raise their own, simply by being in the presence of your higher vibration. So everyone who comes into your energy field has come on purpose, with a purpose, whether you know them or not, whether you notice them or not.

You have so much more influence than you can even begin to imagine! It's why your own healing, your own journey, is so very important. It's why I encourage you to continue to work day after day, to sit with Me in the silence and maintain that connection with all that I am, so you can be all you came here to be.

DAY 199: *Take the Calling*

Tune in! Be present! Hear Me! Listen! Make an effort! And when you hear Me, trust. Trust and act. Hearing isn't good enough if you want this connection to remain open. You have to act upon that which you hear, even if it makes no sense or seems silly, or more especially, even if it makes you fearful. Move forward in spite of your fears!

Some will say to you, "Well, if you are truly acting on God's behalf, there is no fear." And I will say to you, that is just not true. *That is just not true!* What *is* true is that sometimes the fears will be even bigger than you've had before because I will be asking bigger things of you. But I will never ask anything of you that you are not capable of doing. I will not ask anything of you for which I do not provide everything you need to accomplish that which I am asking you to do.

So even if you don't know how you're going to do it when something is asked of you, even if you don't know where you're going to get the resources to make it happen, if it is guidance—if it feels like you are being called—take the calling! Follow it! Because what you need will show up. Saying yes and acting on that yes will open a gateway for Me to put the pieces in place to give you what you need.

But until you take action, the gates are closed. There is no need to open the gates if you are not going to take action, and so I wait until you act. Then the gates open, the pieces move and things begin to shift. New opportunities show themselves.

DAY 200: *Crack Open When Necessary*

The acorn could not grow into the tree if it did not break apart in the earth and allow the water and the nutrients of the soil to penetrate. There must be a cracking open in you also to allow that which needs to enter, to enter, and to allow that which needs to leave to be released. It is just as much a part of your existence as it is that of the acorn.

But you are human and so you feel the pain of the cracking open. You feel the release. You experience the sorrow, the distress. Some of you experience the loss of who you are and wonder if you will ever know again who you are. It's all part of the journey.

It will happen time and time again as you continue to shed the old and become more of the new, the bigger, the more expansive. There is just not one cracking open; there is one after another after another after another. Sometimes the "cracking opens" are big. Sometimes they are tiny and you barely know you've opened until you see yourself doing something different or saying things differently, or perceiving things differently, and then you begin to realize something has shifted.

Sometimes it doesn't seem like the shifting is for the better because it's been a hard cracking open, a hard letting go. Sometimes it will be years hence until you can see the blessings that have come to you because of the cracking open.

DAY 201: *Look Deeply*

What is it you are afraid of finding that keeps you from looking deeply? You say you do not know how. You ask, "How do I get there? What will take me there?"

All that is required is that you spend time in introspection, in silence. Make time to connect with the Divine Source within you, and let that Source *show* you what next needs to be revealed and healed. There is no great effort required, just simply consistently *being* with Me, setting aside time for just you and I to connect. No talking is necessary—no entreaty, no pleading, no prayers—just simply being in that quiet space and saying, "Here I am. Be with me." And I will be.

I think that you think it needs to be more difficult; because you think it must be difficult and time-consuming, you convince yourself you don't have the time to do it. Yet, when you *take* the time, when you *make* the time, when you *find* the time, you recognize there is then time for everything else also.

DAY 202: Make a Space to Hear

The work is yours to do, but you don't have to do it alone. We are all here to help you, all of us who are in spirit. Do you have any idea how many people are standing behind you just waiting to serve you? Spiritual beings, family members, ancestors, angels, guides, all with their own wonderful gifts and strengths and abilities are waiting. But until you ask, until you start to move, all they can do is stand in line and wait. And you can't just ask once and then quit asking. You have to ask each and every time a choice has to be made. You ask for guidance. You ask for direction. Then you wait and listen and make a space to hear our answers.

So often you stay so busy talking that you can't hear anything we have to say, and you wonder why there are no answers to your prayers. It's not that there were no answers; it's simply that you didn't hear them and somehow it caused you to think we didn't care, that you were alone, that you were separate somehow.

When you ask us for help, it's important to make a space to receive that help, to hear the guidance and the direction. Sometimes the help doesn't come in quite the form you might expect or even like. So you have to be open to saying yes even when that assistance comes in a way that normally you would have resisted, from a person you don't normally have in your circle, or because you've been asked to do something outside your comfort zone. There are so many ways we offer assistance.

If you only knew how many times we've offered and you've said "No." You're not even aware of how many times you turn us down.

DAY 203: *Feel Your Divine Flame*

Put your focus on your heart space. As you do so, breathe into your heart space and see the Divine flame that resides there begin to burn more brightly with each breath. That Divine flame is you and Me combined. Breathe into it. Fan the flame. Let it get as big and as bright and as bold as you are willing to allow it. Your breath determines how big the Divine flame within you grows. I am putting you in charge and giving you control. Breathe into your heart space and fan that flame.

Know that as that flame burns brighter and grows bigger, you are saying yes to Me in an even bigger way; you are surrendering yourself to that Divine task, to the spiritual essence of yourself.

Let the flame become a fire. Let it become a bonfire! Let it grow and grow and grow. See the flames shoot higher and higher and higher, reaching upward. As those flames reach higher, know that I am digging more deeply within you. I am unearthing and excavating those parts of you that need to be excavated so your foundation is firmer and you are more whole. I am taking from you that which is incongruent with your highest and greatest good, that which is no longer serving you, that which is holding you back, that which is keeping you small.

As the flames burn higher and I dig deeper, feel your vibration rise. Feel that heat, that flame, the warmth of that flame, the encompassing heat of that flame, move throughout your entire body, burning up anything and everything that is inconsistent with you being your best self: old messages, old beliefs, illness, dis-ease, doubt, fear, woundedness, pain.

I am working deeply and completely. There is no end to what I can make happen for you. So just give Me permission to work as deeply as I wish.

Feel that heat within you, that flame burning brighter. Feel it going deeply through every layer of your being—all lives, past, present and to come, all dimensions, all planes, all levels—cleansed, cleared out, free of debris. Let your body release it in whatever way it needs to be released. Allow it to come. Allow it to bubble up, to burst forth. Allow it to escape through your laughter or your tears, through your song, through sounds, through your sighs, through your words.

In whatever way it needs to show itself, express it, and know it is safe to release it, safe to let go. There is no judgment. There is no criticism. There is no bias. You are free to let it go.

DAY 204: A Request from Your Guides and Angels

Do you remember the emptiness, the loneliness, the aloneness that pervades your being when you are separate rather than in communion? Open your heart always, to everyone, to each other, to those you know and love and to those who are strangers.

Send forth beams of love that emanate from *your* heart, and the *One Divine Heart*, to all those you are with, to all those you pass by. Do this time after time, with person after person, and see the changes that will occur in yourself and in them.

Do as we ask and see what transpires. Do as we ask and feel the difference. Do as we ask and be more of who you came here to be. You are loved, and we are grateful for your presence.

DAY 205: See Gratitude from a Bigger Perspective

If you do not know the bad, how can you appreciate the good? If you have not sat in darkness, how can you appreciate the light? You need to think of these things as you go through your days. Look for the things you can shine your own light upon, your own *gratitude* light. Instead of cursing the fact that you have a flat tire, be grateful for the person who helped you change it or the person who showed you how to change it yourself. Be grateful for the fact that you could!

So many things you can be grateful for if you open your eyes and look at them in a different way. Allow yourself to see the beauty that is in the world, the *purpose,* the rightness. Granted, you have to do this from a bigger perspective. If you have a narrow view of what is good or what is right, or what ought to be, it will be that much more difficult for you to find all the things there are to be grateful for.

DAY 206: Keep Taking the Steps

You have to do *your* work. You can't set an intention then sit back and say, "Okay, God, it's up to you!" That's not how things work. That's not how they work at all!

It's a co-creative effort. Your actions and My actions co-create the outcome. I'm not asking you to move mountains. That's *My* job. I'm asking you to take the baby steps and the big steps *you* can take, because there *are* baby steps you need to take, and there *are* big steps you need to take. I'm not saying giant steps. I'm only saying big steps. And yes, there will be times when giant steps are necessary. Leaps of faith will be required, but you'll be able to take those leaps because you've made the baby steps. You've taken the big steps and you've done the intermediary steps between the baby steps and the big steps. You have seen that as you've taken each step, I have taken steps also, and there have come opportunities for you to move in bigger and better ways, easier ways.

Sometimes your movement puts barriers and blockages in the way and it makes you wonder if, indeed, this is the right path. What you need to know is that the blockages and barriers are the lessons that will teach you what you need to know so when it comes time to take the leaps of faith, you have what it takes to take them.

I'm not going to expect you to jump a chasm when you've never stepped over the crack in the sidewalk; baby steps, growth, moving upward, bit by bit, piece by piece.

Sometimes there will be a bigger distance between one step and the next than there was between the last two steps you took. Sometimes you'll take a couple of really big steps and the next few steps will look like baby steps again. It's all in the Divine plan of how things work and what needs to happen, and how it's all supposed to be.

Trust. Cultivate trust and faith and connection.

DAY 207: A Personal Invitation

I'm waiting for you. I need you as messenger, as instrument. There are so many who would listen to the wisdom you have within you if you would but choose to share it, not just with a small group, not just with those you feel safe with. Shout it from the rooftops, not caring about those who aren't ready to hear, but making it available to anyone who is.

That's your purpose here. I can't put you on the soapbox. I can't put you on the stage. I can only tell you that if you choose to stand up, if you choose to open your mouth and speak out, I will give you the words you need, each and every time, and they will fit perfectly.

The choice is yours. I'm making the offer. I'm extending the invitation to you personally. I don't know what else I can do. I hope that you respond.

DAY 208: *Pay Attention to the Details*

I encourage you to stop struggling and just allow yourself to be present to that which you know you need to do. Listen. See. Hear. Acknowledge and accept the guidance that comes to you.

Look in the details for the information you need. Don't expect the messages to come as some big, booming voice or a banner displayed where you cannot miss it. Look in the tiny, tiny details of life, each daily choice. Pay attention to the details and act upon what you see.

Even the slightest movement forward has value. Even if that slight movement is only *recognizing* that it's time to move forward— not actually moving but just *recognizing it*, because for so long you have denied it. Let that be your first step, that recognition, then pat yourself on the back for recognizing that you recognized it. That can be your second step. See how easy that is? Each time you take a small step and recognize you are taking it, you will be more able to take the next bigger step, and you will do that just as easily as when you took the small step.

Yes, there will be times when you will be asked to take even larger steps—leaps of faith, as they are called. Of course, you've heard of those—and you hope and pray you are never called to take one because you're not sure you'll have the courage. Know that if you do take that leap, if you take the leap you are being guided to take, your heart will sing in a way it has never sung before, and your life will be filled with passion and joy and laughter.

Don't be afraid of the leap. I don't ask you to take it unprepared. Look in the details for the little steps you will need to take to be prepared for the leap. Then just leap . . . and trust . . . for I will be there, arms outstretched, ready to catch you, ready to guide your footing, so you land softly and easily and gently, ready to move forward.

Just pay attention to the details.

DAY 209: *You Are Worthy*

I use those who are willing. You may have asked yourself if you are worthy. You may have said to yourself, "I am *not* worthy!"

And I say to you, as long as you are *willing,* you are worthy. This is what you need to know.

DAY 210: *Make the Best Choice*

Where are you going next? So many ask the questions: "Where am I supposed to go? What am I supposed to do? What will it look like as I am moving along the path? What will be waiting for me at the end of the path?"

What I say to you is this: The path, the journey itself, is what is truly important. How you walk the path determines where you end up. So, as it stands now, there is no ultimate destination for any of you.

The destination will show itself depending on the choices you make, *every choice*—from whether or not you brush your teeth each day, to what foods you put in your mouth, to whether or not you *own* your mistakes. *All choices are equally important*, even though to you, they may not seem that way.

With each choice you make, your destination may change somewhat. Some of you will think it is the biggest choices that will make the biggest change, but that is not always the case. Sometimes it is the *tiniest* choices that you make that will have the biggest outcome in your life. The difficulty is that *you don't know* which choices cause the biggest outcome. So it is important that when you make a choice, you make the very best choice you can make at the time you make it.

DAY 211: Never Doubt

I love you. Deeply and completely from the bottom of My heart, I love you. Never, ever doubt you are loved.

DAY 212: I Am in Love

Do you remember what it's like to be *in* love, when everything is bright and perfect, and no matter what the other does, there is nothing they could do that would turn you away from them because you are so *blindly in love* that you cannot even see or recognize the faults? That's Me in love with you.

But then, that first blush goes away, and there is *true* love, *deep* love, which recognizes the imperfections, the flaws, the faults, and loves you *inclusive* of all of those, without *finding* fault or making a judgment; simply accepting.

I am in love, *and* I love. What more could you ask of Me? How much better could it get?

Can you now begin to love Me the same?

DAY 213: *I've Answered Your Prayers*

You have heard time and time again that I answer every prayer. And you have looked back and thought, *Huh, you didn't answer that one. I didn't get this. I didn't get that. You never helped me here.*

I would ask you to look at those things differently, from a bigger perspective, a wider perspective. Look at where what you *did get* took you, even though your prayer wasn't answered in the way you wanted. The results of your prayers brought you to where you are now, so you needed exactly what you received, in exactly the form you received it, because there was an important lesson you needed to learn from it.

Without that lesson, however it showed up, whatever is still coming for you would be more difficult for you to handle had it not been for *not receiving* what you wanted when you thought you needed it.

DAY 214: *How Long Will You Wait?*

Time is passing, passing much more quickly than you anticipated, more quickly than you know. And yet, you wait. How long will you wait before you take the next step?

You know you are being called. You've had that knowingness for a very long time. There's a yearning in your heart to be more, to do more, to show yourself in a different way. Yet you are holding yourself back.

What are you waiting for? How long will you wait? Will you wait until it's too late? For when a door opens, there is often a time limit to its availability. It doesn't mean there will be no other opportunities, but it will mean the opportunity that was available through *that door* is no longer yours to take.

Think about what's holding you back. Think about why you are putting on the brakes instead of stepping on the gas. Ask yourself if that is really what you want to do. Is this *really* where you want to be? *Is this all you came here to be?*

DAY 215: Focus on This Step

There will be learning experiences along your journey—challenges, bumps in the road, ruts in the road, fences you will have to climb, barricades you will have to break down and walls you will have to disassemble brick by brick.

Do not expect an easy time of it. *I never promise easy.* I *do* promise that whatever you need will be provided. Whatever tools you need to work on the walls and the barricades, to fill in the ruts, to help you over the humps, all of those will be provided, one by one, as you need them, and in ways you probably couldn't have imagined.

But if you focus on what *might* happen, on what *could* occur if you take the next step, it will frighten you. And you most likely will be afraid to take the next step in as big a way as you could possibly take it because you are focused on the what-ifs, rather than on the now.

So focus on the now. Focus on doing what you need to do to take the next step, *only* this next one. That's all you need to be concerned about today and *every* day. What do you need to do *in this moment in time* to take you through this step and prepare you for the next? If you do that, the journey will be so much easier, because you won't scare yourself to death by thinking about what might happen in the future.

DAY 216: *Allow Yourself to Be Uncomfortable*

Step out of the box you have put yourself in. Step out and allow yourself to be uncomfortable. Allow yourself to be *excited* about the uncomfortableness, knowing the uncomfortableness is a sign of going bigger, of being greater, of accomplishing more! It isn't a sign of failure or lack, but a sign of all that is *to come*—a good sign, a fortuitous sign, a sign that lets you know you are doing *exactly* what you need to do.

When there is no discomfort, you are taking no risk. When you are taking no risk, there can be no growth. Growth only comes when you take a risk, when you take a chance, when you try to do something that, to others and maybe even to yourself, seems quite impossible. And yet, you take the steps to make it happen anyway.

To your amazement, and perhaps the amazement of everyone else, it works in *incredible* ways! And it may work in ways you don't even expect: an outcome you couldn't see, an outcome you couldn't imagine, an outcome that perhaps you didn't want because you didn't know that outcome was possible! And yet, it is the perfect outcome that came from the steps you took.

DAY 217: *I Want You to Succeed*

Why are you afraid of Me? What is it you think I will ask of you if you surrender yourself to Me? How can you doubt that I would ask anything of you and not give you all you need to perform the service that I request of you?

It would be a foolish task indeed, for Me to set you up to fail, to ask you to do something and not provide you with all the resources you needed to be a success. I would not do that to you. I want you to be your best, to succeed in all you do in the way that you need to succeed, to fulfill your own dreams and desires for your time in this life.

DAY 218: *You Extended an Invitation*

You know, without a doubt, why you have chosen to travel with the people you are traveling with. You asked them to travel with you and they agreed. You asked them to help you heal, even though the journey would be difficult, and they said, "Yes!" And you said, "Thank you!" *Remember this!*

Remember this each and every time you see yourself, or feel yourself, or think yourself, or know yourself to be a victim. Remember you are simply a traveler on a journey that *you* set the course for, that you invited others to participate with you on. So it is impossible for you to be a victim.

You are a co-creator of your journey, a co-creator of your experiences, a co-creator of your healing and your *un*-healing, your ease and *dis*-ease. You are manifesting what you need to manifest in this lifetime, on this journey, so your soul can learn what it needs to learn to *continue the journey* from this lifetime on.

DAY 219: *Think of Yourself as a Snowball*

Take baby steps at first, of course, but eventually, leaps of faith. Others will say to you, "Where did you find the courage to do that?" And you will say, "I don't know. I just did it. And it worked."

You and I will have *co-created* the outcome. You had the courage to make the choice, to take the step, and I backed you up. That's how this all works. There is a Divine matrix connecting us all, and a Divine momentum that occurs when you take those steps and make those choices, one by one, consistently, time after time after time. It's like that snowball rolling downhill. It gets bigger and bigger and faster and faster, and it picks up bigger things than it ever could have picked up if it had stayed that tiny little snowball at the top of the hill.

Think of yourself as that snowball, rolling, picking up speed, picking up bigger things to do, and having bigger outcomes because of that Divine momentum. You won't be creating; you will be *co-creating* with everyone else that is part of the matrix. And amazing, miraculous things will come to you that seem (with your human, logical, rational mind) not to have been possible in any way, shape or form. And yet, they showed up! They're here, right in front of you.

DAY 220: *Get Out of Your Own Way*

Opening . . . it's all about opening and possibility, so many possibilities! Where is your heart calling you? Where can you better use your gifts in ways that will touch more lives, influence more people, and help others to open up to their own opportunities, their own gifts? That's what your heart wants to do.

Don't you think it's time to get out of your own way?

DAY 221: Tell Me What You Need

What do you need to hear from Me to be enabled to take the next step? Do you need to hear Me say I have faith in you, that I trust you? Do you need to hear Me say that I love you and will always love you unconditionally, without judgment, without criticism, without bias? What is it you need from Me?

Tell Me, in plain, straight language. And if you're not sure what you need, then perhaps you need to spend a little time going within and figuring it out. Because if you don't know what you need, how can I give it to you?

DAY 222: An Explanation from Your Guides

When you make a choice that appears positive, we support that. When you choose something where the outcome seems to be negative, we support *that*. It's the only thing we can do because we gave you freedom of choice and we have to allow the response to be dictated by the choices you make.

It isn't happenstance. It isn't accidental. There is a synchronicity that happens in every instance in your life, a connection between every choice and every outcome that is integral to the entire journey.

DAY 223: *Use Us*

I am persistent, and I am patient. I am loving and kind; I am non-judgmental. I am all the things you need Me to be to help you become all you came here to be. So use Me. Use Me and all of the others in spirit that are waiting for your requests, waiting for you to ask for help, for guidance, for wisdom, for direction.

Use us, *all of us.* You don't have one or two or three or four who are helping. You have legions and legions and legions standing behind you, all with different gifts, different abilities, different spiritual specialties to help you at certain times with certain things. There is no lack of knowledge or information or assistance.

When you're at the highest point on the mountain, or the deepest point in the chasm, when you're somewhere in the middle, or in the middle of all the shit, ask for help. You don't have to say, "Oh, I'm not at the beginning of it. I should have asked at the beginning. It's too late now." *It's never too late to ask for help.* Never too late to ask for help.

We are never too busy to assist. And you don't have to worry that because you need so much of our time, we don't have enough time to give to others. We have an *infinite amount of everything!* No matter how much you need from us, we have just as much and more to give to the next, and the one after that and the one after that and yes, even the one after that.

So take *all* you need, every single little bit. Take it all. Ask for it. Use it. You deserve it. You're entitled to it. It is yours for the asking. And know that we give it with love. We give it with love . . . *unconditional* love.

DAY 224: You Need to Say Yes

You and I are working together. We are co-creating this new you. You don't have to do it alone. No one is asking you to. Sometimes you think you have to do it alone, and you don't ask for help; then *of course* the journey is more difficult. Perhaps sometimes you're not asking because you do not trust I will answer. Perhaps because in the past, no one has been there to answer, to help—no human person, that is.

We in spirit, we are always here and ready to assist, waiting for you to invite us in, to say yes, to ask for our help. Some of you are good at asking, but after you ask, you close yourself off to receiving. Sometimes it's because when we offer our assistance, it comes in a way that isn't what you want it to be, isn't what you expect. So you decide it can't possibly be the answer to your request because it doesn't look the way you wanted it to look. Then you say, "No" instead of "Yes!"

Some of you, when you see there *is* the promise of help, the possibility of healing, become so frightened of who it is you will be when that has all taken place, so frightened you might not know what to do with yourself in this new form you have once that healing is complete, that you step back and say, "Ah, no, no. I'm not ready yet. I'm sorry. I made a mistake. Not yet, not me. It's for that other person. It's not about me, not this time. Maybe later."

It's all about saying yes to being open, saying yes to receiving. It's all about stepping up and stepping forward *after* you have opened up and received; doing what you can do to empower the change, which then gives Me permission to empower *you* in an even bigger way. Again, we are then talking co-creation, *co-creation*.

DAY 225: *I Provide All the Tools You Need*

For some of you, moving forward brings feelings of fear—fear that you will lose the connections you have, the familiarity of you being who you are—and this fear may make you reticent to let go and move on. Remember that fear can as easily propel you forward as it can hold you back, for it is a powerful force.

Remember, you would not be guided to move forward if I were not prepared to provide you with all you need to do so. The tools you need, the support you need, the arms you long to rest in, are all here for you as you allow yourself to take the next brave step and move forward on your path.

I encourage you to step out in faith, knowing you are connected to and loved by a Divine Source that is always and forever present to your needs and desires. As you have faith and step forward, your faith will grow as the path continues to be lit for you. As you continue the journey, your trust and faith will grow, as will the Divine Light within each of you.

I ask only that you have faith. Trust and believe as you take each small step. For at this moment, at this place in your life as in every moment, it is only the next small step that you need concern yourself with. Be present in the moment, on *this* step, and let Me take care of the next.

You are loved and supported in ways you know not, but are there nonetheless. Go forward in peace. Go forward in love.

DAY 226: Find Opportunities to Give

You came here to be of service. You came here to grow. You came here to become more. You can only become more if you *do* more. So stretch yourself! Ask yourself what *more* you can do. If you aren't doing anything to help others at this point in time because you've been so focused on the lack in your own life, I'm going to ask you to stretch yourself in bigger ways and begin to give something in some *different* way than you have given before.

In the process of giving, be totally present in the moment, not caught up in your fears, not waiting to see what will be coming back to you. Just be present in the moment of giving, whatever it is that you're giving: your time, your attention, your money, your space, your presence, your touch, your laughter.

Laughter! Isn't that a funny thing to say? But has anyone ever told a joke and you held back your laughter? For whatever reason, you didn't give them the benefit of your laughter. Maybe you didn't think the joke was funny enough. Or maybe you didn't think you should be laughing in that place or time, that it was inappropriate, and so you held back your laughter. They put the joke out there, they said something funny, and there was no response. They were left feeling empty, and maybe even a little foolish.

So give your laughter. Give your tears. Give a shoulder to cry on, an ear when someone needs an ear. So many things you can give that aren't about money. You just have to be willing to give them. You have to allow yourself to *see the opportunity for giving*. And then to take the opportunity when it is presented: carry a neighbor's groceries, help an old lady out to the car.

What can you do? What can you give? How can you be more?

DAY 227: *You'll Receive What You Need*

I ask you to keep in mind that some of the things you *think* you need are really inconsequential for your journey, and so they will not come to you, no matter how much you request them, because it is not what you *need*.

But *all you need to move forward*, all that will help you and assist you to go through this part of your journey in the most beneficial way, will be available to you. Notice I did not say "the *easiest* way." I said, "*the most beneficial*."

DAY 228: *Confront Your Shadow*

"The shadow knows." You've heard this said so often. "The shadow knows!" *Your* shadow knows. Your shadow knows what needs to be healed. It is doing whatever it can do, whatever is in its *power* to do, to bring what needs to be healed to the surface, so that you are aware healing is needed.

Open yourself to the knowing. Don't slam the door shut and run away screaming! It will find you. And the results, most likely, will be less pleasant than if you had just approached your shadow self head on, with a willingness to confront that which needs to be confronted, to heal it.

DAY 229: *Assistance Is a Blessing*

Some of you still think you have to do it all yourself, that you cannot ask for help, should not ask for help, and cannot accept the help that is offered.

Do you not understand that when assistance comes to you, it is a Divine blessing and gift? *Everything comes from Me.* I am the Divine Source of All That Is. Anyone who offers you assistance is offering you *My* assistance. What you do with it is up to you.

There will be benefit in receiving and benefit in denying, for you will learn from both of those choices. Some of you are so convinced that if you don't have to work at it, it's not worth anything. To conceive that moving forward and moving higher could be an *easy* thing is just beyond your ken. No way, no way at all, can you see that as possible. And yet, with assistance, with trust and faith and following the steps that are lighted for you as you continue on, it really can be simple—not always easy, but simple.

DAY 230: *Make Room for the New*

Keep in mind that I cannot bring something new into your beingness if there is no place for that something new. If you continue to hold onto the old and there is no space for the new, I'm stuck and then so are you. So what are you willing to let go of?

Sometimes you can start by cleaning out your closet, looking through and getting rid of the things you haven't worn or even looked at in years and years and years, because those are old things holding a space; they are old energies tied to an old you.

When you clean out your closet, it's like cleaning out your spirit. You're making space, getting the energy moving. If I were to tell you to start clearing out some of your friends that don't fit, well, that would be a pretty tough place to start.

If you start with your closet, or some other easier way of clearing things out (maybe you've got to start with the junk drawer in the kitchen), you're sending a message to the Universe that you're willing and ready and getting started. Once you start, amazing things begin to happen!

DAY 231: *Your Imperfections Are Gifts*

There is no part of you that is unlovable. There is no part of you that is imperfect. There is no part of you that is less than and no part of you that is greater than. You are unique among all others and your uniqueness makes you special. But that does not make you better than anyone else. It makes you equal to every other being, for you are all special and unique unto yourselves.

I love you for who you are, for that uniqueness, that specialness. I love you when you feel unworthy and when you feel as if you are standing on the mountain top. I love everything about you. How could I not? I have created you just as you are, so *of course* I created you perfectly.

The next time you find yourself talking small about yourself, criticizing yourself and judging yourself, ask yourself what those things you are criticizing came to teach you. What lesson did you ask to be taught through those gifts you call imperfections?

When you can start asking those questions on a regular basis, that which you judge will fall away. That which you criticize will cease to exist, because as you see the lesson you've come to learn through those things, their need to be seen as imperfections will cease to be.

DAY 232: *All Is Well*

This is a time of peace and growth, a time to rest in the stillness of your heart and allow all that is within your heart to be present to you.

Allow your dreams to surface, your hopes to rise. Allow the wellspring of healing that is deep within you to come to the surface to be recognized and acknowledged.

Allow that which you have been struggling with to go free; *set it free.* Bless it and give it wings that it may rise from the depths of your being and be transmuted into the thing of beauty it longs to be.

Be present to all that comes to you from all sources and know it is coming now for a purpose, even if that purpose, that reason, is unknown to you. Trust there *is* a reason and healing is taking place.

Give thanks for that which you have been given and that which is on its way to you. Trust all that comes is exactly what is meant to be.

Go forward in peace. Go in love. Go in faith. You are loved and *all is well!*

DAY 233: What Are You Waiting For?

You have to start somewhere, so start small and work up to the bigger steps. As you take each and every step, I will have your back. I will support you. I will be there to guide you, to lead you, to direct you, to hold you up if needed.

But understand, I cannot take the step for you. Taking the step is up to you. My job is to support you once you take it. So what are you waiting for? Who are you waiting for? What has to happen within you, around you, for you to take that step?

If you're waiting for something outside of you to change

before you can take the step, then what you're doing is giving your power to that external thing, whatever that thing is. You've convinced yourself you can't take the step until your husband or wife approves, or until you're making more money, or until your right foot stops hurting, or your back no longer aches, or until you get a new computer. Oh, wait. You need a new car, and then when you get that new car, then you'll be able to take the step. How long will you wait? How many excuses will you find? How many logical, rational reasons will you convince yourself there are to keep yourself stuck?

You can find many, many reasons to stay small, but is that really what you want? Is that really who you want to be? Because I will tell you, *you didn't come here to be small!* Somewhere along the way, you've picked up messages. You've taken on other people's beliefs or ways of being. You took them on as your own to keep yourself small. At the time you took them on, it was probably to help you stay safe because you knew no other way to stay safe at that moment in time.

But you're not that person any longer. You're grown up. You're in charge of your life. You're in charge of your choices. Even though there are times when you convince yourself otherwise, *you really are in charge of your choices!*

DAY 234: Know This

Be at peace and know that I am with you. I hold you as a new mother holds her new infant, marveling at its beauty, its perfection. I hold you with so much love and gratitude for all you are, all you've been through, and all you came here to be.

I love you. *I love you.*

DAY 235: Recognize the Bearers of Gifts

Recognize that each who comes to you is a bearer of gifts, and that you, in turn, are a bearer of gifts to each of them. Whether they recognize it or you do, is of no consequence.

Sometimes the gifts are invisible, unrecognizable, unknown. It is important to trust that in just your coming together, gifts are exchanged. Whether you recognize how or what doesn't matter; just *trust* an exchange is occurring.

It doesn't take an hour. It doesn't take 45 minutes. It can be the *briefest of seconds* in which the two of you connect. It could be eye to eye, it could be hand to hand, shoulder to shoulder. It could be vibration to vibration as you pass one another on the street. But believe Me when I tell you, an exchange *has* occurred, and it is for the best of both of you.

DAY 236: Sit and Allow

The answers are all within you. You just have to go within and find them. Quit being so busy with the external that you forget the internal.

It is the internal that will open the doors to the external for you. Have you not yet figured that out? That quiet time, that silent time, *that time* will open the inner doors of the Universe to you and will give you access to the Universal energy, the Universal mind, the Universal intelligence—that connecting flow of energy that gives you access to knowledge and information and wisdom that otherwise you would be bereft of. But that connection only comes when you sit quietly and allow the connection to happen.

If you feel something is missing, if you feel like you are having difficulty putting the pieces in place, I encourage you to remember the importance of going inward, sitting in the silence, in the quiet, in the stillness, and just allowing; allowing what's supposed to come to you to come to you. And it will, if you sit in the quiet and allow it.

DAY 237: It's Time for You to Decide

Now is the time to decide which way you want to go. Nothing is, as of yet, set in stone, so the choice is yours. Are *you* making choices, or are you allowing yourself to be buffeted and moved by *others' choices*, by circumstances rather than by desire?

Do not fear you will end up somewhere you are *not* supposed to be. As you have already heard, wherever you end up is exactly where you are meant to be to learn that which you still need to learn. But what is it you need to learn *now*? Is it, perhaps, to put *yourself* first; to decide truly what it is *you* want and then take the steps to make it happen?

You teeter on the edge; you teeter, and you teeter, and you teeter, never backing away from the edge but never taking that next step. You are afraid of the abyss, the chasm, uncertain that what you need will be provided if you step off the ledge. This is a time to trust, to have faith that I and all the others who are here in spirit just waiting and longing to help, will do so when you step out.

Until you take that step, our hands are tied. So what is it that *you* want? Where is it that *you* want to go? Who is it that *you* want to be?

DAY 238: *Let's Have an Intimate Relationship*

Come to Me now. Come closer to Me now. Surrender yourself to Me more deeply now. Let us be connected in a much more intimate, profound and personal way than ever before.

What do you need Me to know? From the bottom of your heart, from the core of your being, what words do you need to speak to Me? What do you long to tell Me, to share with Me? I am here, and I am waiting.

My mind is open. My heart is open. I have no judgment, no criticism. I have only love for you, so pour your heart out to Me. Tell Me your deepest secrets, your greatest fears, your biggest dreams and wildest desires. Share them all, every last detail!

I am the container for all you wish to release. I am the container for all you wish to be held in sacred space. I am all that no one else can be for you. All of that and more, am I.

DAY 239: *Get Out of the Way*

Can you just take a breath and say, "Yes!"? Just put one step in front of the other. Don't worry about what's coming. Don't think about what you need to do to get to the next place. Take care of *today*. If you take care of today, I will take care of tomorrow.

You taking care of today says to Me, "I am ready and willing to move." When you take care of what you can take care of, then I'm left to take care of what there is for *Me* to take care of. But *I* can't take care of anything if you don't move. I have to stay where *you* are. I can only do what you allow Me to do. When you stay still,

I have to stay still with you because we are partners. We are co-creating, you and I, so I can't create anything you are not intent upon creating *yourself*.

But once you say yes, I can take you higher and bigger and better. I can expand you more. You, in your humanness, will be thinking there are so many things you *can't* do; you are limited. In your thinking, you can't imagine how you could do them *yourself*, so you think they're impossible. But if you continue to do what it is you *can* do, then I can work through you and with you and in you and around you. That which you thought was impossible can happen in the blink of an eye, and easier than you could ever have expected, easier than you ever would have conceived possible!

Often things happen and you call them miracles. But really, it's just getting out of the way of the Divine. It's just surrendering to all that is, so you can become all you came here to be.

DAY 240: *It's Up to You*

Whether or not you take that next step is up to you. I can't force your foot forward.

I will, however, support you when you take that step, whatever it is. Even if you choose to stay exactly where you are, I will support *that*.

DAY 241: *Choose Differently*

You say you want your life to be different, and yet, time and time again, you make the same choices. You put yourself where you are by continuing to make the same kind of choices over and over again.

The only one that can get you unstuck is yourself, and that only occurs when you make a *different* choice. Pay attention to what it is you are doing, time and time and time again. You *know* it is not the best choice and yet feel yourself incapable of making a different choice.

Understand, you are *not* incapable. You are simply *choosing* not to make a different choice.

You are the one in charge of your choices. *I* am the one in charge of *supporting* you when you make your choices. So every choice you make, I *have* to support, even if it would not be *My* preferred choice for you.

DAY 242: *Become Your Own Significant Other*

I love you deeply. I want *you* to love *yourself* as much as I love you. Love yourself like a mother loves a new infant. That is the kind of love you need, the kind of love you deserve: nurturing, support-ing, sustaining.

Think of the new infant who, without the love of the mother, would wither and die. That is what will happen if you do not love yourself sufficiently. No one else can love you in that way. If you are seeking that love from outside of yourself, you do yourself a disservice. You sit and wait, hoping it will show up from someone on the *outside*, when the only one who can love you enough is the person *you* are on the *inside*. You are *so worthy* of loving yourself in that way. Yet, no one ever says that to you; but I am saying it.

Perhaps it would be even better if I said to you, "Love your-self in the way you want *another* to love you." Perhaps it would be easier for you to recognize what it is then, for each of you has in your mind's eye a picture of what it would look like to be loved, ideally loved, by a significant other in your life.

Think about what you would want from that significant oth-er, how you would want to be cherished and nourished and loved and pampered. Then become for yourself the "significant other" in your life. For when *you* learn to treat yourself with love and with grace, you will attract others who will do the same, and those who are already in your life will see the benefits you derive from loving yourself like this. They will ask you your secret. *They* will want what *you* have. You will be a role model and a mentor for them, so you're not doing it just for yourself. You are doing it for others, too, but you must start with yourself.

DAY 243: Treat Others as We Treat You

Trust and know that in your desire and wish to be healed, we would not bring you anything that will be a disservice to you. We bring only that which will ultimately benefit you and those you love, as well as those who surround and pass by you. Trust in this and remember it as you go through the uncomfortable time of acclimating to the changes within.

Remember as you change and heal and grow, those around you must also change, for they can no longer dance the old dance when you are dancing a new one. Your new dance may (and most likely will) cause them a measure of discomfort and dis-ease, for they were comfortable in their old dance.

View their discomfort, their moods, their irritability with detachment. They will work to drag you back to the you they knew before the changes. It is safer and easier for them to drag you back to the old ways than for them to move forward into the new ways. After all, you were the one who took the step forward, not they— not consciously, at least. They were dragged along by your strong desire to heal; they were caught in the wake.

So be patient with them in their dis-ease as we are patient with you. Give them the same love and support we offer you. Stand back and watch in amazement and wonder as life begins to hold more joy and more excitement, and you are once again caught up in the rapture of all that is before you.

DAY 244: *We Will Manifest Together*

What would it look like if you surrendered? Who would you be if you surrendered? See, that's the question, and that's what scares you because you don't know who you will be.

What happens when you surrender and change? What happens to your family and your friends and your support system? Will they gather round? Will they support the new you? Or are you afraid they won't be accepting, that they'll turn their backs and walk away; they'll make fun and jeer and call you names, call you crazy?

So many people are still stuck in their own pain, their own woundedness, and when they see someone rising from the ashes, they want to find a way to bring them back down. You have to be strong. You have to stand in your power. Embrace your gifts. *Embrace Me.* I will get you through. You and I together, we will co-create this new you. We will help you manifest all you came here to be and do.

When you surrender, you also need to surrender your expectations, because where I will take you is probably not where you expect to go. And yet, along the way, I will give you everything you need. When you look back, you'll be able to see how all of the pieces fit together perfectly. You'll be amazed that where, once before, you had to go from A to B to C to D and so on to get yourself to Z, when you and I travel together? You will start at A and end up at Z, and you'll be unaware of how you ever got to where you ended up!

In the grand scheme of things, it will look impossible, unlikely, improbable. Yet, we will manifest it together.

DAY 245: *Patience Is Your Friend*

I believe in you. Do you believe in you? Are you ready to take another step, a new step, a bigger step? Because when you're ready and you begin to walk forward, I'll be there for you, and so will legions and legions of others—all of those who are helping all of those who will be coming to you. They all long for you to be your best self because they know the ones *they* are helping need you.

But we are patient, and you should be too. There is no rush. There are many doors opening and closing, revolving and evolving. There is a Divine alignment that must take place in order for that which is yours to do to show up.

When you begin to think things aren't going well or the way that you planned, I want you to remember what I have just said. You can do every single thing you can do, and when the door still doesn't open, it's because all is not yet in alignment for you, and we are working. We are always working.

Patience is your friend right now, even when you chafe against it, patience is your friend.

DAY 246: *Prepare Yourself*

What you think you know is not what you know. What you need to know is still buried within you because you are not yet ready to hear it. It's not anything for you to worry about. I'm simply telling you the way it is so you have a better understanding of where it is you are, and a knowingness that something—some additional guidance or wisdom or direction—is coming to you; but at a later time, when you are ready to hear it, to accept it.

Do whatever you need to do to ready yourself: meditate, journal, pray, jog. Mow the lawn. Dig in the dirt. Sit in the sun. Let what old energies are stilled buried within you come to the surface. Allow yourself to acknowledge them, to face them, and then to embrace them and offer your gratitude. In doing that excavation, you will strengthen your foundation and help make yourself ready when it is time to step up and step out.

DAY 247: *I'm Always with You*

I watch your pain, your suffering, and your tears and My heart aches for what you are going through. If you think, for one small minute, that I would not like to reach down and hold you in My arms and comfort you and take it all away, well, you are grossly mistaken.

I can't do that for you, though, because what you are going through, what you *have* been through, you have *chosen* to go through because there was something in the experience that was of value, and *will* be of value—if not in this lifetime, in the next, because we're not just talking a human being here. We are talking about a soul, a soul that needs to have experience, a soul that needs *all sorts of experiences* to grow and become even more.

So when there is pain in your heart, I am suffering with you, not watching from outside. I am there *with you*. When you are in the depths of depression, I am with you. When your sadness seems to be so great that you will never find the bottom of it, I'm with you there, too. I am also with you in your greatest times of joy; happy *with* you and *for* you. In the greatest moments of your success, when you have the courage to step forward in a bigger way than you've ever stepped before, I am with you. There is not a single phase of your journey that I have not accompanied you on.

I walk beside you. I walk behind you. Sometimes I walk in front of you to clear the path so you can *see* the path. And other times, other times I carry you because you are not strong enough to walk yourself.

DAY 248: We Signed a Contract

I will not ask you to say yes and then give you something you cannot handle. Nor will I bring you a life of chaos and frustration, hurt and pain because you said yes. But understand, when you say yes, what you are saying yes to is that contract we signed, you and I; that contract when you were in spirit and sat with Me and all of your teachers and said, "These are the things I want to learn."

As your teachers and guides, because we love you, we looked at what you said you wanted to learn and for some of you, we said "Yes! Yes! Go forward! That's wonderful!" For others of you, we nudged you to say, "Let me learn a little more!" because what you were setting for yourself were goals we knew would be too easy for you to attain. And for others, we said, "Maybe put the brakes on a bit? That's a heavy load for this life! A heavy load!"

But remember that gift I gave you, the gift of choice? Well, if you didn't heed our wisdom, our guidance, our advice, and decided, like some strong-minded teenager, that you knew best and better, you may have set yourself up when we signed that contract for a life that seems to be filled with chaos and hurt, trepidation, anger, and resentment.

Because of the contract and because of your free will, your choice, I am bound by that contract to give you what you said you wanted. Keep in mind your journey is to figure out how to do what you are doing in a way that raises your vibration, not lowers it. That means even though there is chaos, even though everything around you seems to be falling apart, you find a way within you to be peaceful and calm and centered. You find a way to trust that everything you need is within you.

These are big lessons we are talking about. But we wouldn't be having this conversation if you were not ready for the conversation. You have asked for this information. You needed a reminder. You needed a kick in the butt, and so here I am, giving you what you asked for, even though you might truly not have known exactly what it was you were asking for. But you knew you were asking and I'm glad you're here.

Your presence shows Me you are ready to grow again. It shows Me your willingness to be cracked open in a different way; your willingness to let go of old ways of being, old beliefs and old messages. It shows Me you are ready for change, upward movement, and a higher vibration.

I am very, very grateful you are present here today.

DAY 249: *Do This with Intention*

Take a few deep, deep breaths. Feel the breath coming in and going out. Notice any areas of your body that are feeling tight or tense or are calling your attention to them. Breathe into those areas and let the breath, as you breathe it in, heal those areas.

Bring those areas of dis-ease back into ease and grace. If you breathe into one area and it becomes an area of ease, and another area pops up calling for your attention, breathe into *that* area. Pay attention to what your body is telling you, sharing with you. Pay attention to its wisdom. Pay attention to its desire to show you the areas that need to be worked on where you are holding those old messages and beliefs. Give yourself an opportunity to release those by breathing in the higher vibrations and breathing out the lower.

Such a simple exercise, but so powerful if you do it with intention. You are your own best healer.

DAY 250: Delete "Mistake" from Your Vocabulary

Know that whatever choice you choose, I am supporting you in that choice. Remember, too, to detach from the outcome of the choice. Have no expectations of what will come as a result of the choice you make. Be as detached as possible from the outcome. If you expect one outcome when you make the choice and another presents itself, know the other outcome, the manifestation of your choice, is *My* choice for you based on what I know you need, what your soul needs, to help you learn what you need to learn to prepare you for the next step that is coming. That is why I say to you the word "mistake" should disappear from your vocabulary.

It is only when you look back at what you have done—and the outcome was not what you expected from the choice you made—that you label what has happened a mistake. I'm asking you now to understand that the outcome, the manifestation of that choice, especially if it was not the outcome you expected, was a blessing from Me. And, yes, there will be times when you are challenged to see the "blessing" in the blessing, for it may appear to be one of the most difficult things you have had to do in your entire life.

There may be fear, there may be tears, there may be doubt, there may be loss, but there will also, somewhere within the experience, be a truth you needed, a gift you needed, or a blessing—perhaps even a joy, if you can look deep enough—that will serve you well as you walk forward.

And if in the midst of whatever is occurring, you are unable to spend the time to find the blessing, just trust there is one. I bring nothing to you that you have not agreed with Me upon before it ever occurred, for we are co-creators in this life you are leading. So first, keep that in mind, and secondly, remember I bring nothing to you that does not serve your highest and greatest good.

DAY 251: *Use What Works for You*

Who am I, you might ask. I am whoever *you* need Me to be: healer, confessor, mother, father, brother, sister, husband, wife, loving and accepting nurturer.

I can appear as the little boy down the street with freckles all over his nose and curly red hair, or the loving and accepting grandmother, hair pulled up in a bun, always wearing an apron, cooking your favorite food or baking cookies. I can be the doting father, the loving mother. I can be the best friend. I can be your guide, your mentor, your teacher. I am all those things and many more besides.

However you need to see Me, however you need to perceive Me to enable you to draw closer to Me, is how I want you to perceive Me, to see Me, because I want nothing more than to have the deepest, most intimate relationship with you it is possible to have. And I can't do that if there is anything about Me that frightens you or causes you to fear Me or doubt Me.

See Me however you need to; call Me by whatever name works for you. And it does not have to be a holy, sacred name. You can call Me Ralph or Henry, or Josephine or Delores. You can call me Susie, Tommy, Teddy or Kerry. *I don't care what you call Me.* If it helps you to call Me a Divine name, so you feel that I am more rather than less, do *that*. But if calling Me a Divine name scares you off or makes you feel you are less than worthy, or someone has told you that you have no right to speak to Me so intimately, then perhaps calling Me

Ralph or Susie or Diane or George will make it easier for you to speak to Me more personally.

Who I am, what I am, what I can co-create with you, will not change regardless of what you call Me, or how you perceive Me. However, if you perceive Me as less than who I really am, it may cause you to believe I cannot bring to you all that you need, that I cannot *be* all you need. I encourage you to perceive Me, to put a face to Me, that brings you in and draws you closer rather than puts distance between us, because I long for closeness, for joining, for connection, for harmony.

You are special to Me, each of you, and I long to know you in the most incredibly personal, intimate way you will allow. The more you let Me in, the more assistance I can be, the more comfort I can provide.

I am asking you to let Me *all the way in*, to trust Me in ever bigger ways, to let your faith grow, expand and be more, in all ways, on all levels, all planes and all dimensions.

DAY 252: Go to the Depths

I know you want to avoid the depths, but you cannot avoid the depths and still experience the heights. They are both ends of the same spectrum, so when you close yourself down on one end, you close yourself down on *all aspects* along that spectrum.

As much as you wish to avoid the pain, the hurt and the sadness, as tightly as you clamp yourself down to keep from going to the very depths, the very pits, when you do that, you've also then eliminated any possibility of going to the greatest heights.

I promise you, *I promise you*, if you are willing to go to the deepest depths, I will take you to the highest heights. You will see, *you will know to the very core of your being*, that whatever happened to you in the depths was well worth it for your experience now at the very peak of all that is. You can only experience this, though, if you trust and go where I lead you in all ways and at all times.

DAY 253: *Go Forward in Integrity*

I'm not asking you to do anything special. I'm only asking you at this moment to be your best self, to be in integrity, to be accountable; to be above board and honest in all your actions, not only with others, but with yourself. How often, how often do you fool yourself into believing something? How often do you make excuses? How often are you less than honest with yourself, because if you were completely and fully honest, you would have to choose differently?

It's impossible to change something you don't like about yourself, or something you wish was different, if you don't accept where you're starting from. When you look at yourself with honesty, with integrity, with love, and you begin to work to raise your own vibration so you are your best self, your true self, your authentic self, every single person whose energy your energy touches has the opportunity to move higher also.

Think about how many people you touch in a day . . . physically touch in a day. Now think about how many people you speak to in a day. Think about how many people you look at in a day. Think about how many people you pass by every day. Now understand that each of those people you have just taken note of has been impacted by your vibration. And all of the people *they* think about, they talk to, they see, they touch, *all of those people* whose energy they walk through, are now impacted by you also because they were impacted by you. And it goes on from there.

Think about yourself. Wouldn't you rather come in contact with a higher vibration, a vibration of love rather than a vibration of anger or impatience or hatred? Think about what happens when someone comes into your energy field and they are angry or upset. What happens to your energy field?

Think about the difference you can make if everywhere you go, you go with the intention of being your best self, your highest vibration.

DAY 254: Consistent Action Makes a Difference

Watch for the messages. Listen to the guidance. Say yes instead of no, and once you say yes, don't take it back. Then begin to do what you need to do to move forward, whatever little steps call to you.

Begin somewhere, in some part of your life, moving forward. As that shift happens, it will impact other areas of your life and you will find yourself moving forward in a number of different ways on a number of different levels. As you keep saying yes, you will see things pick up speed, and that which you thought would take three weeks to manifest, happens in a day and a half, and in miraculous ways you couldn't even have begun to imagine.

It's not up to you to determine how I do My work. It's only up to you to say yes and do yours.

DAY 255: It's All Part of the Plan

Your gifts are many . . . many yet still undiscovered. You've received glimpses. You have ideas. But there is so much more within you.

Pay attention to what you're receiving. Pay attention to where you're being led. Do not be surprised at where the guidance takes you, which may be totally different from where you think you are headed. It is all part of the plan we have for you. All part of the plan you set in motion when you incarnated into this lifetime, into this body, into this beingness.

Know that all is in perfect and Divine order. Just follow the steps, one at a time. Revel in them. Embrace them. Learn all that each step has come to teach you and then learn from the next and the next and the next. What you will do with that learning will become clear when it is needed. Until then, just trust in the process, and in us.

DAY 256: Now Is Your Time

This is *your* time, not My time for you; *your* time for you. And only you can *own* this time for you. No one else can make it yours. They can take it away from you if you don't own it completely. You can *allow* them to have that kind of control over you if you are afraid to step up and honor your own heart.

But if you can honor your own heart, you can *own* this time and this space, completely and fully and entirely. And what comes to you because you have honored that space will be *amazing*!

It won't always be easy. You'll have to take some risks. There are always risks when you move forward. *Always!* But when you honor your own space, your own time, your own heart, your own needs, then what comes to you from that honoring will be *true* and *real* and *honest*. And *exactly* what you need for where you are.

So honor yourself. What is it that *you* want now? What is it that you need for yourself? What is it that your heart craves and your soul longs for? What is your gut screaming for? What is it that you've been reaching for, for so long?

Now is *your* time.

DAY 257: Accept Yourself

Stop judging yourself and start accepting yourself exactly where you are, as you are. That's not to say that if you want to be more, or something different, that you shouldn't keep working. But it is saying you should be okay with who you are now, because who you are now is perfect.

DAY 258: *We Respond According to Your Intention*

Some of you believe that when you pray to Me, when you talk to Me, when you ask something of Me and it does not come in the way you determined it should, that I have not heard or answered your prayers.

I want to remind you that you are holding Me to a higher obligation. Before you came into this lifetime, you told Me there were certain things you wanted to do, certain lessons you wanted to learn, certain experiences you wanted to have. You counseled with Me and all your guides, all your teachers, all of the angels and spiritual beings who are here to work with you. And there are many of us who work with you, who work with each soul before it takes on the implication of another physical existence.

We give you our best counsel. We say to you, "No, no. This is way too much for you. You're not ready for this!" Or we say, "You know, we think you could take on more." Or, "You know, we think you've chosen wisely." But if you do not agree with our counsel, because you have been given freedom of choice, we must honor your decision. *We must honor your choice.*

And then? Then we sign a contract with you. We sign a contract that says we will hold ourselves accountable to the lessons you want to learn and we will be responsible to this contract, and to you. That means there are times when you ask for things and expect them to show up in certain ways that they will not appear—not at all or not in the way you require—because they don't meet with the contract you had us sign.

It would be so easy, wouldn't it, if you all remembered that contract? If you all remembered why you chose this journey, these particular experiences, this particular lifetime. But if you could remember, there would be no challenges in doing what you are doing in this lifetime, would there? And so there would be no learning and no reason for the lessons.

We, we are all asking you to trust that we hear every single prayer, every request, every conversation you offer up to us. All are responded to in the way we know is best according to what *your* intention was when you came into this existence.

DAY 259: Share Without Attachment

Put forth your own wisdom from a place of detachment. Offer it without being attached to what others will do with it. Your work is to share what you know, to admit what you don't, and to acknowledge those who may know more in some areas than you do.

DAY 260: *I Know What You Need*

All is right. All happens because you've asked for it to happen to help you grow, to help you become more, to help you be the best you came here to be.

These are not coincidences. They are synchronicities. Look at them and see how they are connected, one to another, the past and the present.

As you move into your future, continue to look behind you and see the connection from all that was to all that is, and know that all is taking you exactly where you are going in the way that is best. Have no doubt, I *know what you need!*

DAY 261: *Repeat It Until You Learn It*

Love, laughter, joy, peace, hatred, anger, doubt, discomfort, illness . . . all are necessary. All are a part of the fabric of human existence. You travel through all the emotions, all the experiences, learning as you go . . . or not.

If there is a lesson you came to learn and one experience does not help you learn the lesson, you will repeat the lesson time and time and time again until you learn the lesson you came here to learn. And I want to be clear about that for you. It is not a lesson *I* have chosen for you. It is a lesson *you* have chosen for you.

Your spirit, your soul, decided this is what you needed when you came into this human incarnation. So there have been experiences set up for you to ensure you have an opportunity to learn the lessons you came to learn.

It doesn't always mean you'll learn the lessons in *this* lifetime, that you'll complete the learning. Sometimes you'll try over and over and over again and still not learn the lesson. It is just what it is. There is no wrong or right to that. And yet, you will assign judgment. You will criticize yourself. You will call yourself wrong or insufficient. You will see yourself as lacking or less than because you are continually doing it over and over and over again.

What I would say to you is that each time you have an experience in which it seems you are repeating the same lesson, you are learning *nuances* of the lesson—the bits and pieces intrinsic to the knowingness you will ultimately come to, whether in this lifetime or another.

Nothing is wasted; nothing is without purpose. All are necessary for your growth, for your healing, for your moving forward, for your eventual expansion.

DAY 262: Whose Voice Are You Listening To?

Who are you? Who do you want to be? What's holding you back? Why are you choosing to stay where you are? It's your choice, you know. Nothing can keep you stuck unless you want it to, unless you give it the power. Aren't you tired of empowering something that's holding you back?

What old messages are you listening to? Whose voice is that in your head telling you that you can't, telling you you're not good enough, telling you you're too old or too young, you don't have the right degree or the right certificate? Whose voice is telling you that you don't know enough, that you're not enough?

Somewhere along the line, you bought into those old messages. Somebody repeated them often enough that you began to believe them, especially if they were people who seemed to love you and care about you. Do you understand they were speaking from their own hurt, their own pain, their own woundedness, and what they were saying to you was really how they felt about themselves? *It had nothing to do with you!*

But if they could point their fingers at you, they wouldn't have to turn their fingers and point at themselves. If they could look outside, *outside of themselves*, they wouldn't have to look inward. So it wasn't that they wanted to hurt you; it wasn't that they wanted to keep you small. It's that *they felt small*. They were hurt. They were wounded. They passed their woundedness off on you because they didn't know what else to do.

When you were young and you first heard their messages, you didn't know that you didn't have to accept them. You didn't understand why they were coming. Perhaps until just this very moment, you didn't have that understanding, but you're an adult now. You don't have to buy into anyone else's message. You don't have to own what other people say about you. You can tell yourself who you are and what you want. You can replace those old messages with whatever new messages you choose.

DAY 263: Rent a Two-Year-Old

Each of you should rent a two-year-old for a day and busy yourself with the activities that attract a two-year-old. Let yourself *be* a two-year-old *with* that two-year-old, not the parent *watching* the two-year-old!

Be the two-year-old! Become the two-year-old's playmate for a day. When was the last time you picked up a crayon and colored? Or picked up a paintbrush and just played with the colors to see what would come when you mixed them all together?

Why is it you've forgotten to take time to play?

DAY 264: You Are Worth It

It is important as you move forward to heal yourself in the best way possible. You need to be as healthy as possible to be the best channel for the highest vibration of energy I wish to bring through you. There are so many, *so many* who can be a channel for vibrations that are like cold water running through their veins. It is easy to do that. Your vibration doesn't have to be very high at all. But if I want to bring vibrations through you that vibrate at the temperature of molten lava, how many of you are in the best physical shape to allow *that* to happen?

How many of you say to yourself, "Oh, tomorrow I will do it. *Tomorrow* I will eat healthier. *Tomorrow* I will quit smoking. *Tomorrow* I will stop using drugs. *Tomorrow* I will lose weight. *Tomorrow* I will exercise." It's always tomorrow and somehow tomorrow never comes!

I'm asking you to love yourself enough *today* to make different choices for your body. I'm asking you to love yourself enough *today* to treat yourself the way *I* would treat you if I had total control over what you did within your body and outside of your body. That's how I want you to love yourself, because you are worth it. *You are worth it!*

DAY 265: Divine Reason Is at Work

Give up needing to know where you are heading; *give up needing to know*. For as I have said time and time again, even if you think you know where the path is leading you, nine times out of ten you will end up somewhere different, because where you thought you were going was where I let you *think* you needed to go just to get you moving.

If I had shown you where you were going to end up when you started the journey, you would have been too frightened to start because what you would have needed once you got there was more than you currently had. Had I shown you the end at the beginning, you would have convinced yourself there was no way possible for you to get there. You would have gotten in your own way, and in Mine as well, and tied My hands because once you believe you can't get there, I am unable to help you in the biggest way I desire to make that leap possible.

So understand that when you think you know the ending, or think you know where you are going, there is *Divine reason* in what you are seeing, *Divine reason* in what you are knowing, *Divine reason* in what you are hearing. I encourage you to open yourself up and take the step, but without expectation as to where you are being led, accepting that you could end up exactly where you see yourself, or nowhere near where you see yourself, and either will be the best for you at that moment in your journey.

DAY 266: *Hold a Higher Perspective*

You do not have the power to pick and choose the spiritual helpers we send your way. Those in spirit? Many have been assigned to you for life after life after life. And those we bring to you in human form? They are those who have agreed to act as your teachers, your helpers, your mentors, your companions; and so they come to you as part of the package, just as you are part of their package and their learning. *You come together to serve one another!*

I ask you to hold this higher perspective. For some of you it may be difficult, especially if you feel yourself a victim, if there is what you call in your life a perpetrator. You have for so long seen yourself as a victim that to think of yourself as a co-creator of your journey, even of those things that have been so harmful, so difficult, so challenging, makes you shudder to think you would co-create such a situation. Yet, I ask you to remember it is not your *human self* that created those situations. It was your *soul*, before you incarnated, that took it upon itself to learn these bigger lessons, that you, in your humanness, have no memory of choosing. That is why it is so easy to feel you are the victim.

It's important that you hear this different way, this different perspective. Allow yourself to explore it, to think about it, to understand it, to take it in, and hopefully, to accept it as how things really are.

If you can see yourself as a co-creator rather than the victim, you will move through each of the challenges in your life in a very different way. You will seek to find the answer; you will seek to find what the challenges have come to teach you. It is a different way of being in the world, and from My perspective, a much easier one, if you can embrace it.

DAY 267: *Exist in Love*

Fear or love . . . those are the only two paradigms you can exist in. The more often you choose from love, the easier it is to choose from love. And the more often you choose from fear, the harder it is to get away from fear.

Fear is insidious. Once it grabs hold of you, it takes over. It takes you down the rabbit hole, and it is so, so hard for you to bring yourself back up out of that rabbit hole.

So exist in love, *always love*. As much as it's possible, *choose from love*.

DAY 268: *Be Self-Loving*

It's time you stop trying to please everyone else and please yourself instead, not because you're angry or fed up, not because you're full of rage or resentment, but because you love yourself enough to know you need to treat yourself better. *You need to love yourself more.*

Put yourself first from a place of love. When you do that you are better for everyone around you, including yourself. It isn't selfish. When you love yourself first, what you then give to others is of better quality. Now what you're probably giving is quantity, but the quality? Probably not so good.

I'm sure many of you have been taught that putting yourself first *is* selfish. I'm going to challenge you to think differently; to begin to understand and believe that putting yourself first is self-loving, at least when you come from your heart space, from a place of love.

Selfish? Yes, if you are coming from anger or resentment. But *self-loving* if you are coming from a place of love, of knowing this is what you need to do to be your best self, to reach your full potential, to be all you came here to be.

DAY 269: *I Desire Your Presence*

Presence, *your presence* . . . I desire your presence in a more consistent and intentional way.

Be with Me, be with all of us who are here to help and assist you. Give us the opportunity to do *for* you and *within* you that which we long to do. Do not shy away from us. Embrace us! We are many and there is much we can do to assist you on your journey.

So sit quiet and listen. Sit quiet and be present. Talk less and listen more. Surrender your will. Give us the opportunity to work *through you* so Divine will may triumph over human will, so Divine light may shine where human shadow resides, so healing may occur at an even deeper level and we may take you higher than you have ever dreamed.

Be present now!

DAY 270: *Own Your Oneness*

You get too caught up in the hustle and bustle, the going from one place to the next, the doing of this, the doing of that, the fear of not doing enough, the fear of lack, of not having enough. You push yourself to do more and more and more. You find your worthiness in your doing and forget you are worthy just simply because you *are*.

Sit quietly in the sand, or on the grass, or in a field of flowers and just *be present*. Just soak it all up. Know that wherever you are, whatever you are doing, you and that which is all around you are one. Allow yourself to *own* that oneness. Allow yourself to be present. Allow yourself to breathe.

DAY 271: *Drink from the Divine Fountain*

Allow yourself to drink from the fountain of the Divine that is within you! You do not have to search outside of yourself. *I . . . am . . . within . . . you!*

Taste Me. Try Me. Drink *from* Me and *of* Me. Let what flows *through* Me fill *you* up, perhaps in a way you have never felt filled before.

You do not have to sip lightly from this fountain. There is no end to what comes from this eternal spring. You do not have to be afraid of what's offered here.

Drink deeply. Drink often! Come back again and again and again and again! Not to some external place, but to the *internal* place of your being where I am present: in the center of your heart space. That is where I reside. That is where I always am!

DAY 272: *It's a Conundrum*

Because we are One, both of us must take the step together. I cannot go where you will not lead Me, nor can I *lead* you where you are not *willing* to go. It is a conundrum, I know, but it is as it is.

Be brave. Be courageous. Take a risk. Step out of your comfort zone and into your power zone! Be all you came here to be. Be all I know you to be.

DAY 273: Be Brave

Sometimes you have to be brave for the others who cannot, even when being brave means you have to step so far out of your comfort zone that you want to travel backward as far as you can away from that next step and pretend it was never shown to you.

But that next step has been shown to you because I knew—*I knew without a doubt*—that you could take the step, so I lit the step for you. I made it a possibility. And understand, I said a *possibility*. It is not an order or a command, not a directive. I am not saying, "This is what has to be." I am saying, "This is what is possible if you are ready."

But I *am* saying, if you take that step, everything you need, in one way or another, will be provided for you . . . *everything!*

DAY 274: It's All Up to You

When you take ownership, responsibility, *accountability* for your choices and your actions, you empower yourself. When you look inward instead of outward, you are able to make the changes you say you desire to make.

As long as you continue to point the finger in someone else's direction, how can you even begin to take responsibility? You are not responsible for their change or their growth or their diminishment!

You cannot make them change so you can change in accordance with *their* changes.

You can, however, change yourself. By doing so, you give them an *opportunity* to change as they come into resonance with your higher vibration. But you have to say "Yes!" instead of "No!" You have to say "I" instead of "you."

You have to look inward instead of outward. You have to move forward instead of back. It really is *all up to you!*

DAY 275: We Can Have a Personal Relationship

What you need to see, you will. What you need to know, you will. What you need to hear, you will. I'm asking you to trust the hearing, to trust the seeing and the knowing that comes to you, because it isn't that the messages don't come; it's that you choose not to see or hear or know them. You don't trust that there *are* messages.

You don't believe you are worthy of hearing them. You don't trust that I would want to talk to you so intimately and so personally. Or perhaps someone has told you it isn't possible for *you*, as just a mere human being, to actually connect with the Divine intimately and personally!

Perhaps someone told you there needed to be a priest or a minister or a rabbi that acted as mediator, as go-between, between you and that Divine Source of All That Is. And you, because that message came at such an early age, you believed it. You bought in. Because you lived with that belief for so long, for so many years, hearing it over and over and over again, it is rooted deep within your being.

So sometimes at a point in time when you most need to hear Me, what comes up is that old message telling you that you're not good enough to talk with Me directly, that you can't possibly be hearing the voice of the Divine because it just doesn't work that way!

Sometimes, because you're scared of taking the next big step, you choose to allow *that voice* within you to take prominence rather than the smaller, quieter, more loving voice that says, "Yes, you can! Here I am! Come be with Me."

DAY 276: Don't Go Down the Rabbit Hole

You are in control of your thoughts and emotions. Most of you find that hard to believe. Many of you don't want to be responsible because if you *are* responsible, it means when you have thoughts and emotions that are not "positive" or "the best", *you* have to take responsibility for changing them; *you* have to be accountable. It's so much easier to think it's out of your control because then there is nothing you can do except be a victim of your own thoughts and emotions.

I'm telling you, you *are* in control. It's just that you have to be aware of what you're thinking, aware of what you're feeling, and you need to *choose* to think and feel differently. Now, I'm not saying that if something happens and you feel sad, you shouldn't feel sad. I'm saying that you shouldn't *wallow* in the sadness. Allow yourself to feel sad. That's the human experience you came here to have; but if you allow yourself to wallow in that sadness and allow it to take you deeper and deeper and deeper down the rabbit hole, *that's a choice you're making.*

Choose not to go down the rabbit hole. Choose to think differently about the experience. Choose to think positively, hopefully. Choose to think from a place of love rather than fear or anger or hurt.

DAY 277: *The Reaction Matches the Action*

I'm asking you now, from this point forward, to work harder than ever before to choose higher-vibration choices more often than not.

Vibration attracts vibration, so when you choose the higher vibration, you attract the higher vibration. When you choose the lower, you attract the lower. No punishment—never a punishment—just the outcome of your choices.

For every action, there is a reaction, and the reaction matches the action.

DAY 278: *Make Your Choices Wisely*

This fast-paced life you lead will continue to pull you further and further away from that which can bring you the greatest joy unless you make a direct and conscious effort to do otherwise. We ask you to make that choice, to be fully conscious of your choices so each choice is made with the highest and greatest good in mind as the final result.

Each choice, even the smallest choice, has power and importance in the great scheme of things. Just because you do not know the impact of your choices directly, do not for one moment believe they do not matter.

All choices matter. All have an impact. Think of this. Be aware of this. *Make your choices wisely*.

DAY 279: Take the Step You Are Ready to Take

You are free to choose. You can choose to return to that place where you have been for so very, very long, or you can choose to do something different: to take a risk, to take a step, to move out into the world in a different way, from a different place, with a new energy.

It is up to you. And as you have heard us say time and time and time again, *we support every choice you make*, whether that choice is to go back where you were or to venture out into the unknown. We support your choice.

Understand there is no wrong or right. You will take the step you are ready to take, and it will be exactly what you need it to be for the lessons you have come here to learn.

DAY 280: Let the Light In

There's so much old stuff in your past. You guard your heart to protect yourself, not fully understanding that as you built the walls to protect your heart, you've walled in the pain, the anguish, the hurt.

With the wall up, those things are stuck behind the wall. The darkness stays within and no light can enter. Even if you can only take down one brick at a time, it's better than nothing. Let in the first bit of light. Take down the first brick and it will be easier and easier and easier to take down one after another after another.

I can't force you. I *can* tell you that even if you are afraid, life will be better—you will be better—if you can let the darkness out and the light in. Yes, it's a risk, but it's so worth the risk if you're ready to chance it.

DAY 281: *Life Is Better Without Walls*

Sometimes I feel like I have to beat down the walls you have erected. I understand that you built those walls to protect yourself at a time when you knew no other way to do so, but those walls no longer serve you. You have built walls to keep things out. What you don't realize is that they are keeping in the old, the pain, the woundedness, and they are keeping out the healing, the love, the joy and the rapture.

I can't take your walls from you if *you* wish to keep them. Only you, *only you* can disassemble that which you have built. So take the walls down, even if you have to do it brick by brick, bit by bit, piece by piece, because you are so afraid of what will happen if you no longer have that wall.

Life is so much better without the walls. I won't lie to you and tell you there won't be pain or challenges or difficulties because, of course, there will! *That is life!* But along with all of *that*, you will feel the rapture! You will know the healing! You will feel the bliss! How many of you even know what bliss is?

DAY 282: I'm Here for You No Matter What

Some of you have heard Me being called "judgmental." You think "an eye for an eye" literally means an eye for an eye, that I will do to you what you have done to others.

Whether you see Me as father, mother, androgynous, whether I have human form in your mind's eye, or spirit form alone, whether you think of Me as simply energy or a being, no matter how you see Me, I am telling you now, *there is no judgment in Me!* I have never *not* been proud of you!

I have, of course, empathized and sympathized when the choices you have made have taken you down a much more difficult path. But I do not berate you or criticize you or think less of you; nor do I remove My support, although, because of the messages you have heard from others and from things you have learned, you may believe that to be the case.

I am telling you now—*in person, directly*—that I do not do those things. *I am here for you no matter what!* Nothing . . . nothing you do, nothing you think, nothing you say or feel will ever change that. I know that is difficult for you to own because it is difficult for *you* to do for anyone else, but that is because you are human and spirit combined, and you are still learning.

DAY 283: *You Are Divine Perfection*

As you work to heal the warts *you* have, others who have similar warts will look at you and know it is possible for them to move beyond their own warts. You give them hope. You give them a role model. They need you.

I need you. I'm not asking you to be perfect in the human sense of perfection. I'm asking you to be perfect in the *Divine* sense of perfection, and you already are. You just need to accept it; *allow yourself to accept it.* Breathe it in. Own it. Embrace it.

You are Divine perfection, and I love you. I love you. *I love you!*

DAY 284: *Your Soul Needs the Experiences*

It is difficult being spirit and human, one juxtaposed upon the other, trying to work your way through the humanness as your spirit longs to soar and be all it knows it can be. But *it* needed the lessons you are learning here. *Your soul* needed the experiences you have been through, as much as you have hated or detested them, as much as you have questioned the veracity of your life.

All that has happened to you has happened because you have asked it to be so, because you have needed it to be so, for this journey your soul is currently engaged in.

DAY 285: Why Did You Come Here?

You don't have the power to change anyone. *I* don't have the power to change anyone. I can only *support the choices you make*. When you choose to raise your vibration, when you choose to move higher, to dig deeper, to heal more, I support each and every choice you make. Of course, if you choose to stay stuck in your rut, to not move forward, if you choose to keep focusing on the same path, guess what happens? I support those choices, too.

I'm asking you: What choices of yours would you have Me support—those that move you forward or those that keep you stuck? *The choice is yours.* I follow your lead. As you begin to choose, more and more often, those choices that raise your vibration, you get a momentum going, and we pick up speed, you and I. It's like that snowball that rolls downhill. We just keep getting bigger and bigger and bigger, and we include more and more things as we get bigger and bigger.

As *you* pick up momentum, *we* pick up momentum. We co-create in bigger ways, more expansive ways. And our vibration—yours and Mine together—is then able to make a bigger difference in the world. Isn't that what you're all about, making a bigger difference in the world? If you could, wouldn't you rather make a mountain of difference than a molehill of difference?

Really, let's think about it. Did you just come here to be small, to do just enough to get by? Or did you come here to be the best you can be? It's your choice. *It's your choice!*

DAY 286: Stoke the Fire

Imagine a flame burning as brightly as it can burn. That is My love for you! Yet even to that flame you can always add another log to keep it burning brightly, to assure that it will not burn out so My love for you is always stoked. Each and every time you come to Me, you add more fuel. You help yourself believe and know that I am present. It is not that the flame goes out, it is that sometimes you begin to *doubt.*

Sit with Me. Be present to Me. Call My name! Be a part of Me! Let Me be a part of you as often as you can, so *you* are fully stoked and *your* fire, *your* desire, *your* love for *Me* and your awareness of My presence in you, does not die down.

I am in love with you, and I love you. Take that with you as you go forward today, that knowingness, and hold it close to your heart. Hold *Me* close, and let Me work within you and around you, in whatever space you give Me. Know that the greater the space you make for Me to work in you and through you and around you, the more I can create.

If big spaces scare you, give Me a little space to start with until you see how I can work. Then expand the space and give Me more and more and more. What you will see as you look behind you is the *proof* of the work I have done for you. And that proof, *that proof,* will help you move forward in bigger ways.

DAY 287: Congratulate Yourself

I commend you for your courage and strength. I ask you to be as proud of yourself for the work you are doing as I am proud of you. In all honesty, *My* pride in you really means nothing if you have no pride in yourself. For it is pride in yourself that will drive you to take the higher road, to make the higher choices.

Feel good about what you are doing, even the choices that lead to chaos. You are at least moving forward and are not stagnant, not stuck. If you are very, very, very afraid of where those choices may lead, take little steps and make small choices—tiny choices that you know you have the best chance of succeeding at.

As you build your confidence because of your successes, you will have the courage you need to take the bigger steps. Do not berate yourself because you are choosing small steps; instead, *congratulate yourself for taking a step* and not being stuck.

DAY 288: *I'm Sticking to My Promise*

There is no such thing as perfection, but I made you perfect just the way you are, with all the bumps and warts and flaws, perfect for your journey, perfect for what you came here to learn. Without all of the attributes you have, you wouldn't be able to learn the lessons you came here to learn.

The experiences you're having—the ones where you keep saying, "No, no. Poor me. Why is this happening to me *again*?"—they're happening because *you need them to happen* because you didn't learn the lesson the first, second, third, fourth, and tenth time!

And it will keep happening until you learn the lesson. Not because I'm punishing you, but because you told Me before you entered this existence that this is what you wanted to learn, and I promised to help you. So I'm sticking to My promise, even when it pains Me to see you in pain.

DAY 289: *Live from a Place of High Vibration*

We are connected, you and I, deeply, and have always been. There has never been a separation. All you need to do is remember this and open yourself up to the vibrations, those higher vibrations, that are there, deep within your heart. Then live from that place of high vibration.

As you live from that place, it will flow *from* you. Others will feel it. More will be attracted to you and you will bring into your life *exactly* what you need to become more of who you came here to be.

DAY 290: *You Are Uniquely Special*

You are all lightworkers, not just in the sense of energy workers, but in the sense of working with *My* light, y*our* light, *our* light.

You have the ability, the gift, the *talent* to reach out to others, to assist others, to assist yourself. These are not special gifts. *You* are not special, not in the way so many people think of when they say, "Oh, you think you're special!"

You are special because you are unique. Each of you has different gifts, different talents, different abilities. Each of you has a unique vibration. Each of you is necessary . . . *necessary* . . . in order to help the healing that is needed all over the world. Each of you will attract to you those who are attracted by your particular vibration. They are coming to you because they resonate with you. They need you and you, you need them.

They will help bring your gifts more clearly into focus. Some of those who come to you will appear to be your greatest challenge. Perhaps you might even see them as the devil incarnate! Your first instinct will be to push them away. Nay, it will be to run away, to get out of there as quickly as you can, and go as far as you can! Just keep them away!

Be aware of those! Those are the ones who have the greatest lessons to teach you. Those are the ones who will help your gifts expand and evolve into even greater gifts and abilities.

DAY 291: Start Fresh

You can, today, begin anew in deciding how you make your choices. You can decide to choose the *higher* choice, the *bigger* vibration. Perhaps today you can give yourself a clean slate. See yourself as starting fresh, letting go of any judgment or criticism you may have about yourself or the others who are in your life and on your journey with you, giving them clean slates also.

Everyone deserves a fresh start. Let go of judgment and criticism, frustration, irritation, anger. Let go of all those things and let all who are in your life, *including yourself,* have a fresh start.

DAY 292: Take a Breath

It's important for you to take time to breathe and be present. How often do you just do that? How often do you stop in the middle of something hectic going on, when it feels like there is nothing but chaos around you, and just stop and close your eyes for a moment, sixty seconds, and take a deep breath in, and then breathe out, and just pause for a moment . . . and be?

You might be amazed at how big a difference it makes in your life, how much more you hear, how much more you see, how much more you are aware of! Even more of a difference if you do that eight or ten or twenty times in your day! Just for that sixty-second period . . . a deep breath in, a big breath out . . . and then pause . . . to let the world in, to let *Me* in, to say, "Yes!", to say, "Thank you!", to say, "I am present."

DAY 293: Choose to Let Go

Letting go isn't easy, especially when you've worked so hard to hold on. But you can make a choice to let go. In fact, *letting go only happens when you choose to let go.* Will there be some work involved and some discomfort? Yes, but I can promise you, if you follow it through, if you start the process and continue, the rewards will be great. Things will begin to change in your life in ways you can't even begin to imagine, in ways you wouldn't have ever thought possible, because you said yes, because you opened up, because you said you were ready and were willing, because you gave Me permission to step in and assist. It's all up to you.

How far do you want to go? How much healing are you ready for? How much bigger do you want to be? How many more lives will you be able to touch because you stepped into your power instead of away from it?

You can't even begin to know how powerful you are! And you will only begin to know when you are ready.

DAY 294: *Move into the Light*

Step out. Step away from the darkness and move into the light—not an exterior light, but an *internal* light, the light that is within you, *My light within you!* Step into it! Let it shine from within you. Let it light the next step on your path.

As you light the way for yourself, you will also light the way for others, those who are connected to you by familial bonds, by friendship bonds, even those who pass you unknown in the street, even those will feel the vibrations coming from you as you move higher. And unknown to you, you will have *raised* their vibration also. They will be forever changed because they have come into the light shining from within you.

They will not know it was *you* who took them higher but *I will know*. I will know you chose to spread your light, to share it, to give it to others, to allow others to know the healing you have known through the allowing of your gifts and pushing through your fear.

There is *so much good* within you. *I see it.* Why is it so difficult for *you* to see it?

DAY 295: Raise Your Vibration

Beacons of light, instruments for the Divine, messengers, emissaries . . . each and every one of you, *each and every one,* different, unique; vibrating at your own unique vibration, each with your own sphere of influence, vital and important and necessary to all who come to you, all who are around you, all who pass by you.

I need you, each and every one of you. *I need you.* You are the only hands I have, the only human hearts I have, so when you open *your* hearts to another, you are opening *My heart* to them. How many do you know who need a physical representation to believe in Me, to trust in Me, to know that I exist?

You are the physical manifestation of Spirit, Divinely created, perfectly created, to do the work you came here to do, different work for each of you, because everyone needs something different and someone different.

Not everyone will be attracted to you; *you're* not attracted to everyone. You're only attracted to certain people, so you will attract those to you whose vibration is similar, whose vibration you have the capability to raise as you raise your own.

That's what you're here for: to raise your own vibration, to do your own work. As you are out in the community, because of the work you have done on yourself, you are helping others raise their own vibration and facilitate their own work.

DAY 296: *Your Response Is Important*

Every single part of your journey is important, and *how you respond* to the experiences in your life is important. How you respond shows you how far you still have to grow, what you need to learn—if you can see it that way. That's why it's important not to get attached to the outcome, but to be able to stand back when you have made a choice and look at the outcome and say, "Okay. A + B led me to C."

I'm going to tell you that A + B *always* leads you to C. The problem is that C may not always look the way you want it to. But *A + B always leads to C,* just like *2 + 2 always equals 4.* It's just that *2 + 2 can't be anything but 4!*

However, when we're talking A + B = C, well, you'll have an expectation of what you think C will be, and when it doesn't show up? Well, if it looks like less than what you wanted it to be, then it's a mistake. It's an error. You get all bent out of shape. If it comes out better than you expected? Well, you're joyful and gleeful, and it's absolutely wonderful.

And yet, there is no greater miracle in it being better than you expected it to be than in it being less than you expected it to be. The end result was *exactly* what you needed it to be to take you to the next step on the journey.

When you have an experience, when you make a choice, and the end result comes to you, just take a look at that and ask yourself, "Now that I'm here, where do I go next? What's my next best option?" And take that step, and then the next and the next and the next. That's really what it's all about.

DAY 297: *Perfection Is Impossible*

Keep in mind, always, that you are human. You can be so hard on yourself as you travel a spiritual path, thinking that you must be perfect every single moment of every single day simply because you are trying to walk where Spirit leads. *It is impossible for you to be perfect.* You are human *and* you are spirit, and simply the butting of the heads of the two will cause you difficulty and challenges from time to time.

Just rest on the premise that you are doing the very best you can as spirit and human. Allow yourself to be present in the moment. Allow yourself to appreciate *who* you are and *what* you are and where you are going.

Let go of criticism and judgment and worry and anxiety. Just allow yourself to take note of that which happens, how it happens, and work to do the best you can with the next decision you need to make. It is *all* you can do. It is all that I *ask* of you. It is all that I *expect* of you. You are much, much more demanding of yourself than I am of you.

DAY 298: *Think About This*

I am in love with you. I do not simply love you. *I am in love with you.*

I want you to think about the difference in those statements: I am in love, *and* I love you. That "in love" excitement, exhilaration, the "I can't wait to be with you! I miss you so much when you're not here!"? That's being *in love,* and that's how I am with you!

So often the "in love" piece leaves, and you feel love, but it doesn't burn as brightly or as strongly. It isn't as exhilarating. It doesn't fill you with excitement, not like being *in love* fills you.

What you need to know is, I am *both* when it comes to you. I am always and forever in love *and* loving you, so that each time you sit with Me, I am *so* thrilled and excited that you are back! I have missed you *so* much and feel *so* blessed that you have returned!

DAY 299: *Practice Gratitude*

Your life is a miracle, whether you recognize that or not. It truly *is* a miracle just as it is. Appreciating that miracle and being grateful for your life will take you out of the rabbit hole and move you higher.

But practice, *practice* is what you need. Not just one moment of gratitude here or there, but *a practice*. Do it over and over and over and over again, so there are more times than not when you are in gratitude. Then you will really see big shifts and changes, and you will feel the difference within yourself. You will awake each day excited about what's to come, looking forward, eyes wide open. That's the way all of life should be lived!

DAY 300: *Look at Yourself*

Remember, when others are judging you, they are really judging *themselves*, not you. Their judgment has *nothing* to do with you and *everything* to do with themselves, for what they are claiming as a lack in you is really a lack in themselves. It's so much easier for them to turn their focus outward than inward, because then they don't have to look at what *they* are doing. They're so focused on you and your issues that they can convince themselves they have none. Or, at the very least, that yours are worse than theirs.

The same is true of you when you judge another. It has nothing to do with them. *It has everything to do with you* and what you are feeling about yourself. When you see a lack in someone else, it is because you *feel* a lack within yourself. It doesn't matter what the lack is you are seeing. It only matters that what you are seeing as a lack in them is coming from that lack within yourself.

So when you find yourself sharp-tongued, or critical, judgmental, unloving, when you see yourself giving *less* rather than giving *more,* ask yourself what's going on with *you*—not with those to whom you have directed your actions or your thoughts—but what is going on with *you*. What are *you* missing? What are *you* lacking? Why are *you* being judgmental or critical? Why are *you* being unforgiving?

I support whatever you put out there. You need to remember that. Even the tiniest decision you make is supported by Spirit. Sometimes it is what seems to be the most inconsequential choice you make that is really the lynchpin that determines the next direction you are going.

God is in the details. You've heard that said that over and over. Guess what? I am! I'm in the details, but I'm in the mountains, too! I am *everywhere!* And because you are Me and I am you, you are everywhere, too!

So remember when you point your finger at another in judgment or in criticism, you're really pointing your finger at yourself because you are a part of that person, just as I am a part of you and you are a part of Me!

DAY 301: Move On with Love

I need you to shine your light even brighter than you already are. I need you to use that expanded light, that light you have in your heart center, in a bigger way and to do so without worrying about how it will be received, or what others will think of you.

Know that you are doing the Divine work you came here to do. Yes, there will be some who will push you away, who will deny and reject you. That is on them, not you. That is part of their journey. Your journey is to continue to move forward, to understand that when others wound you, when they reject you, it is because of their own woundedness. It isn't because you are not enough.

You need to take that in. You need to allow for that possibility and move on in whatever way you can—not with anger or guilt or resentment, but with love—blessing them, thanking them for the opportunity to allow you to grow and expand in such a way that you can return their rejection with love . . . not a love that makes you feel less than, but a love that lets you walk away feeling whole and complete and knowing you have just touched a wounded heart.

You've been given an opportunity to extend a healing hand, a loving ear, a shoulder . . . and that opportunity was a blessing.

DAY 302: *Your Spirit's Definition of Success*

Walk forward in faith. That's not always easy. But when you say yes, I give you everything you need to succeed on the journey.

Now here's the difficult part: Your definition of success in your humanness may be different from your *spirit's* definition of success. For you, success might be that it's all gone, all that pain, all that suffering. There's no longer financial struggle. Your relationship is finally healed and all is well. But your spirit's definition of success might be that you made it through; you experienced what you needed to experience and you came out the other side stronger, bigger, better and more prepared for the next part of the journey. *That* is really the success you're looking for.

Sometimes that's not easy to take. Be present to what you're feeling. Be present to your thoughts. Be aware of your resistance, your denial. Be aware if you're pushing against instead of embracing. Just be aware.

DAY 303: *Tune into Your Core*

It isn't unusual to clutch at that which is trying to be released, especially if it has been with you for a very long time. Your ego feels comfortable holding onto that old stuff. When you let go of it, there is a space—an empty space—and your ego fears what is coming to take its place, for it is something new and bigger and more powerful.

Just because letting go is uncomfortable doesn't mean you shouldn't. Just because a part of you wants to take it back doesn't mean you should. Tune into your knowingness! Tune into the core of your being, and from that place deep inside of you, discern if it is better to let it go, to release it, or better, in the long run, to hold onto it. Ask yourself. Do not let yourself be dissuaded by your ego. Tune into your core.

DAY 304: *You Are Prepared for the Next Step*

I have not promised you, nor will I ever, that coming closer to Me will be easy. If you could do it in the blink of an eye, *everyone* would do it, because *everyone* wants what I have to offer. Or, at least, they *think* they do, if they think that what I will bring them is riches and power in the material sense.

Following a spiritual path is not for the weak or the cowardly, but you do not have to be the most courageous of people to walk that path. You simply need to have a willingness to take the steps that show themselves to you. Each time you take a step, know that I am providing *exactly* what you need for that step, whether it be courage or comfort, support or humility, patience, assertiveness, strength, persistence or initiative.

Whatever it is you need for that next step you will have, *always*. The only question is whether or not you choose to take it up and use it.

DAY 305: Offer Love

I know you even better than you know yourself, even though you might not like to admit that I do. I know the deepest nuances of who you are, where you've been, what you've done, the things you are *most* proud of and the things you are *least* proud of. I know that which you speak of, and that which you hold sacred and quiet within you because you are afraid that if everyone knew all there is to know, they would turn away from you. They would feel you are unworthy of love. They would call you less than, and you would begin to *feel* less than, and so you hold those secrets to you.

Remember, those who say you are less than say this because

they feel less than themselves. If they can make *you* smaller, *they* can feel bigger. When they call you names, when they walk away from you, when they try to make you feel you are unworthy, it is because that is how *they* feel. That is what is deep within them and they are trying, *trying,* to put it on you, because if they can put it on you, they do not have to look within. That is what is happening.

So I ask that when you hear those words that in the past would have made you feel less than, I ask you to remember the source of the words and the underlying issues for the person who is speaking them. I am asking you, instead of judgment, to have compassion, to come from your *heart space* and offer them love, even if you do not think they could accept your love, even if they do not understand you are offering them love.

What is important is not how they receive what you offer, but that *you are big enough to offer it* from your true heart space. Every single time you offer love and compassion to someone, you affect the energy in the world, in the universe—as well as that one person, whether they accept it or not. You are affecting the energy *everywhere!*

That's how much power you have when you open your heart and allow the love to come from your heart space and generate outside. *You have so much love!* So much power! If you really knew how much power you actually have, you would probably run away. That is why I do not show it to you. It is why I let it grow within you slowly and show itself bit by bit, so you can acclimate to the gifts as they come up—one by one, bit by bit—because I want to *use* you . . . not abuse you, *use* you. And I want you to use what I am bringing through you, not just for your good, but for the good of all who will come to you.

DAY 306: Something for You to Think About

Understand, I have no judgment as I speak to you. There is no criticism in My words, although you may take it as criticism. There's only an attempt to illuminate for you a different perspective, another way of looking at and perceiving what is happening in your life to open you to other different and new possibilities.

I understand, perhaps even more fully than you do, that every single thing you are doing, every single thing you are experiencing, every single thing you are *being,* is in Divine order. So there is no judgment, just a desire to see you grow and expand and heal and move forward on your path as quickly as is right.

Sometimes it takes a reminder. Sometimes it takes another's viewpoint to help you see what's happening in your life; to help you understand that you are allowing yourself to be distracted because *you are afraid of your own power.*

Just something for you to think about.

DAY 307: *Beware of Perfect Teachers*

Teaching isn't just about standing up in front of a room full of people and spouting your wisdom. After all, if you don't *walk* your talk, *talking* your talk is empty.

As you go forward and seek out others to teach you, be aware of whether or not they are completely aligned with what they are saying to you. Do their actions match their words? Or do they say one thing and do another? Do you hear stories about them you can't believe are about the person you know? The person you know, you may only know on the surface because they hide well that which is truly underneath.

Make no mistake, *no one is perfect*, and every teacher will have flaws, *every* teacher. If there is a teacher who seems too perfect, *beware!* That teacher is hiding the flaws, covering them up, pretending. You are human. Your *teachers* are human. And as human beings, none of you is perfect.

But when your teachers own their imperfections, when they recognize they have spoken in error, perhaps spoken in anger or fear, and they acknowledge their response was inappropriate, perhaps hurtful, and they make the necessary apologies and own what they have done? *Those are true teachers.* Those are the ones you want to seek out. Those are the ones you want to emulate. Those are the ones that will help you move higher.

Do not be afraid of imperfection. It, in and of itself, can be a great teacher.

DAY 308: *God Loves Speed*

I love speed! I like to move fast. I like to see things getting done.

It's you humans that drag your feet. You'll get an idea, you start to run with it, it looks like it's going take off and all of a sudden, fear attacks your gut. You dig in your heels. You sit on your haunches. You glue yourself to the fence. You convince yourself that even if you try your hardest, it's not going to work, so why bother trying? Or you begin to think that even if you do what it is you're feeling called to do, it's not going to make any difference in the long run, so what's the point?

You won't know until you try. And there really isn't any *trying*, there's either doing or not doing. You humans have used that "try" word to give you an excuse so if it doesn't come out the way you think it should, you can at least console yourself with saying, "Well, I tried." Because if you say instead, "Well, I did it. I just didn't do it perfectly," then there's one more thing you can judge yourself about.

Quit labeling things. Quit saying good or bad, right or wrong. Just say you're doing it. And however it comes out is how it's meant to come out and is absolutely perfect, whether *you* think it is or not. Obviously, if it needed to be different, it would be.

Understand, there are no accidents. Every single thing you do has purpose and reason behind it. Just because you don't know the purpose or can't find the reason doesn't mean there isn't one.

DAY 309: *Your Timing Is Perfect*

I have said time and time again that we are here to be of service to you, but we can only do that if you are willing and ready to accept our help, if you are willing and ready to move forward. Until *you* begin to take the steps to move you forward, it will be more challenging for you to hear the guidance; not because it isn't there, but because you're not open to it yet.

I'm not trying to rush you. Your timing is perfect in whatever way it shows up. And I'm not impatient with you or frustrated. I know when you are ready, you will open yourself to hear and you will begin to move. There are so many who can use your gifts. Just know they are waiting for you.

DAY 310: See Your Warts as Marks of Grace

You have everything you need to move forward in your life. Don't let anyone tell you otherwise. You are whole and complete and perfect just as you are, even with what you think are imperfections. Those are *not* imperfections! They are *uniqueness*. They make you *who you are*, and there is no one else quite like you anywhere in the universe. They are *not* blemishes or warts; they are marks of your specialness.

Begin to see your warts and your blemishes, your "imperfections", as blessings, as marks of grace! If you view them differently, if you love them completely and without judgment, you will find yourself blessed in ways you can't ever have imagined! You should try it sometime.

DAY 311: The Nature of Trust

Begin to ask the question, "Where am I being led?" Begin to ask for signs that you will understand and recognize. I know your *soul*, but you are human *and* spirit, so consequently what your spirit needs may not be what *your humanness* needs to move you forward. From your *human perspective*, what kind of messages do you need from Me? How best can you recognize them? How are you most likely to see them, to notice them? Tell Me.

Some of you need a voice. Some of you need a picture. Some of you need things repeated time after time after time before you'll take action. There is not one among you who is not already receiving guidance; don't allow yourself to think otherwise! You're looking for excuses *not* to take action. The messages are there, right in front of you. Some of you are unwilling to recognize them, for you know if you do, it means you *must* take action.

Some of you have convinced yourself that you *can't* take action, that you are stuck where you are. You tell yourself that perhaps at some later date you will take action, when the conditions are ready, but not right now. So what's the point in seeing the guidance if you're not going to act upon it? If you're not ready, you convince yourself there is no guidance, there are no signs. And even when something slips into your awareness? You pretend it is just an accident, a coincidence.

What do you think will happen if you follow the guidance? Understand, I will not ask anything of you that I do not provide you the tools and resources to do. That would be foolish of Me, wouldn't it? And who has ever said I am a fool? All knowing, perhaps, all powerful. But never a fool!

I will not ask you to do anything that I am not prepared to prepare you for. The problem is, you want the proof before you take the step. If you know anything about Me and the way I work, often I need you to take the step *before* I provide you with the proof. It is the nature of walking a spiritual path. It is the nature of trust and faith.

DAY 312: Your Journey Is Entwined with Others

Your time is not yet, though you long for it to be. You're aware of certain yearnings within you, things you *think* you should be doing, or *want* to be doing. You're always searching for more clarity. And yet, were you to have that clarity, you would recognize that at this point there is really nothing more for you to do because there are other pieces that need to be in place, and it is not their time yet to be placed. So where you are is where you need to be, and if you would just quit chomping at the bit and relax into being, soon enough there will be *so* much for you to do that you will wish you were back at this point in time.

All is as it is meant to be. All happens *when* it is meant to happen. Your being impatient will not serve you or the others in your life. You chose a path and you are *walking* that path. Your humanness needs to be where it is, even though your spirit longs for more. The two are coming closer and closer together in being what they are supposed to *be* together.

But your human journey is entwined with others, and all those pieces must be taken care of before your sole focus can be on you and the journey you came here to do for your soul's individual purpose. Be patient. We are with you. You are on the right path. Just be patient.

DAY 313: *Let Love Lead You*

I'm not saying you shouldn't be afraid. You are human and fear is part of the human path, the human experience. I'm simply saying *don't let the fear stop you.* Walk forward in spite of it. In fact, *use it to fuel your step.* It is a powerful energy. Harness that power for your good rather than allowing it to stop you in your tracks. Listen to your own internal knowingness. Tap into the guidance. Let the Divine be the guidepost on your journey rather than listening to what others may be saying to you, others who are afraid for themselves and so put their fear on you.

Those who are telling you that you can't do what it is you are saying you want to do, they're not saying that to you because they don't think you can do it. They are saying it because if you take the step, there is no reason they shouldn't take the step they're being called to take themselves, and they are afraid . . . afraid for themselves. If they can convince you not to take the step, then it is easier for them to say they're not ready to take the step. They use you as a rationale for staying stuck, for staying small, for allowing fear to be their guiding force.

Will you listen to the internal or the external? Will you let fear guide you, or will you let love lead you? What is your choice?

DAY 314: *Peel Back the Layers*

Healing begins within you, within each of you. Seek not to heal others when you, yourself, are not whole and complete. Healing is a process, a long process. Step by step, bit by bit, layer by layer, you peel back your fear, your hurt, your doubt, your woundedness.

As you are giving to others you must also give to yourself, intending yourself to heal as you intend others to do so. Without doing the work on yourself, you have less to give those who come to you. You are not as clear and open a channel. Your ego will more frequently get in the way. It will impede My work *through you.*

I ask you, *I urge you,* to work on yourself in all of the ways you have been given the ability and skills to do, not just once or twice or three times, but over and over and over again. Peel back layer after layer after layer until you think there cannot possibly be any more layers, and yet, beneath those layers, there are more, lifetimes and lifetimes more. The higher you wish to go, the deeper you must peel back the layers.

DAY 315: *Practice on the Small Things*

You *need* the person who cuts you off in traffic, the one who steals the last parking place. You need them because they are teaching you patience. They are teaching you how to take it in and let it go without affecting you to the deepest level.

If you can handle those little slights, those little insults? You will be so much better off when it comes to handling the big difficulties, the big problems, because you've practiced on the small things.

DAY 316: *Position Yourself to Receive*

If you're not sure, ask for guidance, for direction. Come to Me, come to all of us who are here in spirit waiting to be asked for our assistance, our guidance, our direction. Lay the question at our feet and then position yourself to receive an answer.

So often you will ask us questions without making a space to hear our response. We appreciate your prayers, but understand that when you are busy talking to us, you can't hear us. If you come to us in prayer asking, questioning, needing guidance and direction, share what you need to share then be silent and listen. Listen with your mind and your heart, as well as your ears. Let that which you need to know bubble up from inside of you. Allow yourself to be present to it, to own it, to embrace it, and yes, to act upon it.

If you get the guidance once and you're not quite sure it really *is* guidance, ask for it to be repeated in a different way, a different form. If it comes again and you're still not sure, ask again. Perhaps you need to tell Spirit how many times you need to hear the message so you'll believe it's really from Source and not from your own self. Give us some guidance, some direction, as to how you need to know for sure that it's for real. We'll provide what you need. We want you to believe and to trust. We want a deeper connection, all of us. There are so many of us here in spirit waiting to assist.

DAY 317: *Be the Catalyst*

Children of the light, it's time. It's time for you to move forward, time to take the step you have been thinking about taking but have been holding back on. It isn't easy to move forward, especially when there are friends and family who are encouraging you to stay exactly where you are, because if you change, they must also change.

You are taking this journey intentionally but they are being dragged behind you, and perhaps they're not quite ready. So as *you* take the step, their egos will kick and scream and throw temper tantrums, working hard to get you to go back to where you used to be because that is the you they know and love and are familiar with.

But you, you have chosen a *different* path. You have decided it is time to move forward, *so take the step!* Facilitate your own healing, your own growth, your own expansion, and by doing so, give an opportunity to all of those who come into your life to follow.

It is their choice. You have no control over what they do with the gift of opportunity you give them. You only have control over what you do for yourself. Some of them may kick and scream, some of them may leave the playing field. Perhaps family and friends who were so close to you and so much a part of your life will suddenly decide they can no longer be with you because you are so different. It is really themselves they are afraid of, not you. You are just the catalyst that might take them out of their comfort zone, and so consequently, they have to push away because they are not ready to leave that zone of comfort yet.

DAY 318: *Learn from Your Choices*

The choices you make determine where you end up. I'm not in charge of your final destination. I'm only in charge of *accompanying* you along the journey. It is up to *you* where you end up, based on the choices and decisions you make along the way.

Each time you choose the *lower* vibration, you change your course. Each time you choose the *higher* vibration, you change your course. Every decision you make, every *choice* you make, changes eventually—in some way, tiny or large—where you *finally* will end your journey in this lifetime. I encourage you to consider that each time a choice presents itself. Ask yourself which road you want to take now: the higher vibration or the less high vibration. It's your choice.

The journey will be different depending on the choices you make. No choice is a *wrong* choice. *All choices* teach you what you need to learn. Obviously, when you choose the lower vibration, it is because there is something from that path you still need to learn.

This is not about berating yourself for making a "wrong" choice, for there are no wrong choices, as I've already said. But it *is* about looking back when you have made a choice that doesn't turn out the way you expected. It *is* about looking back and seeing what the other choice was that you might have made and why you chose *this choice*, so the next time a similar choice occurs, you may choose differently based on that which you have perceived from the journey you have just taken.

DAY 319: *Own Your Value*

How often do you give and give and give of yourself until there is nothing left, and then you give more, without ever stopping to take care of yourself?

It always amazes Me to see how much you continue to give when you are empty! Most of you find a way to pull it off. But did you ever think about the *quality* of what you were giving when you were empty, how effective that assistance really is when your tank is empty, when your vibration is low?

Think about how powerful your assistance would be if you were filled to the brim with energy, if you were taking care of *you*. If you were filled to overflowing so that what you were giving was the excess, not what was left over in the bottom of the pot, the dregs . . . can you just imagine the difference in the quality of your help?

Do you understand—have you ever stopped to think—that sometimes when you say no instead of yes to help someone out of a hot spot or a problem, that you're giving them an opportunity to learn for themselves the lesson they need to learn? Sometimes the only way they're going to do it for themselves is if you refuse to do it for them.

I want you to stop, I want you to stop and think, *really stop and think*, when someone asks you to do something from now on. The first thing I want you to ask yourself is, "Is it in my highest and best interest to do this now?" What you might *say* immediately upon being asked the question is, "You know, let me check my calendar," so you don't have to give an immediate response, so you can go home and sit with the question, "Is this in my best interest?"

If the answer is yes, then do it, but if the answer is no, hold fast to that no. Love yourself enough to take care of you and say no.

You can be honest about it. Those little white lies you tell? Who are they helping? You know, the more of those you tell, the harder it is to get out from under them. There are so many of them that you can't remember who you told what to. So simply be honest and say, "You know, I'd really like to help, but right now is not a good time for me." If they can't hear your "no" in a positive way? If it causes anger or resentment? If they try to guilt you into doing it? Understand those are *their* issues, not yours, and you're actually helping them to deal with them by saying no and holding firm.

So many ways to learn the lessons you came here to learn! So many ways to help others learn theirs! Your journey isn't just your own. It's for everyone who's on it with you: your family, your friends, your boss, your co-workers, the neighbors with the dog that keeps pooping in your yard. They're all here to teach *you* a lesson. They're all here so *you can help them learn their lessons.* You're not alone. You're co-creating every single minute of every single day by every single choice you make.

So I'm asking you to begin to choose more wisely, to start

loving yourself better, to start owning how valuable you are and how much you deserve to treat yourself with love and kindness and respect and gentleness.

DAY 320: Tonight's Homework

If I were to give you homework tonight, I'd suggest you write a list of all the good things about yourself. Maybe right now the only good thing you can say is that you're very, very good at balancing your checkbook, or you always, *always* take the dog out for a walk. Or maybe the only good thing you can say is you always tip well, even if the server doesn't seem to deserve it, because you know they're having a bad day and you want to make their day better.

Whatever it is, put it on the list. Every time you think of something new, add it to the list. Let your list be a work in progress as you look deeper within yourself, as you become more aware of the beautiful and loving and kind person you are. That's the homework I would give you if I were going to give you homework.

DAY 321: What Not to Do

Don't compare yourself to anyone else. Don't point fingers. Don't wonder why someone is so hesitant at moving forward when you are jumping and leaping and skipping ahead. Don't assign blame. Don't say they're not willing. Don't say there's something wrong.

Understand that just as you do, they have their own unique paths and purposes. And while theirs might look different from yours, they are no less than yours, nor are they any better than yours. Different, yes, but equal, and all are necessary.

DAY 322: I Have No Judgement

I have never been human, so I do not know the human struggle except through *your* humanity. As you experience it, I experience it, but the perspective certainly is a different one. And so consequently, I *do not truly know* the challenges you experience in the way you experience them. I can, however, see the suffering you go through, the struggles. I can feel what you feel on some level, but truly not in the way *you* feel it. I can *say* I understand why it is difficult for you to choose the highest choice, but truly, I cannot walk in your shoes.

That is why there is no judgment in Me about the choices you make. I will not judge you because you say no when I hoped you might say yes, or when you say yes when the better answer for you might be no. I can only hold you in My heart and love you completely, without any reservations or limitations or boundaries, without any expectations.

You are free to choose when to say yes and when to say no, when to take a step forward, and when to stand still. And I honor those choices, each and every one of them. No matter how big or how small, I honor them.

We are One, you and I. When you take a step forward, I take it with you. When you stand back, I am there with you also, but never in judgment, only, *only in love.*

DAY 323: Do What Makes You Happy

How long will you keep making the same choices expecting a different outcome? How long will you continue to put yourself in that position, when that position is no longer comfortable or pleasing or bringing you joy?

It isn't easy to step out into a different way of being, but if you want to *be* different, you have to *choose* differently. You have to take different steps. You have to choose your words more carefully. You have to come from a place of loving yourself from your heart space and do what makes you truly happy.

Isn't it time for you to let go of the old ways and step into the fullness of your being?

DAY 324: Work Within to Make a Difference

There is no such thing as two ships that pass in the night—the thought being that they have passed without making a difference, without touching, without being aware they are passing or have been passed. This is truly not the case, for each of you is connected to every other one of you by the presence of the Divine within you. Through that connection, and because of it, even those you pass unknowingly in the street are different because of your passing.

As you continue to heal yourself, as your vibration continues to rise to higher levels and with greater clarity of intention, the differences you will see in your own life and in the lives of those around you will become more and more obvious, and the vibration of your entire environment will rise to match that which comes from *you*. As you heal, they heal. As they heal, the world heals. As the world heals, there can be nothing else but peace.

Work within to make a difference without. As your inner light shines brighter and brighter, your sphere of influence will continue to grow in magnificent and wonderful ways. Those you touch will touch others who will touch others who will touch others; and you will have no way of knowing that the person who one day reaches out to touch you, to offer help or assistance, is only there because of someone you touched long ago who also touched this one now touching you.

Do not allow your fears to stop you. Do not allow the walls you have erected, knowingly or unknowingly, to get in your way. Bring down the walls. Walk outside the walls and allow your light and your vibration to touch all that come to you, all that you reach out to and all that pass by you.

In doing this, you will have done that which you came here to do. So be it, and so it is.

DAY 325: Be Accountable

If you want people to honor the gifts you have to offer, you must be accountable to yourself and true to yourself. You must seek deeper healing. You must be more responsible. You must own when you don't know something, rather than give any answer just to give an answer.

You must be in integrity as you move forward. There's nothing wrong in saying you don't know, even when you are saying to people, "I'm an expert in my field."

Not every expert knows the answer to every question. They will respect you more if you acknowledge you don't know and seek an answer, not only for them but for yourself.

DAY 326: Take Care of <u>This</u> Moment

Just step forward one step at a time. Be present in each and every moment, for it is in being present in the moment that you will be enabled to see and know the next step.

You will have choices on this path, and all your choices will serve ultimately to enhance your purpose. There are no right or wrong choices or right or wrong outcomes. There is only what is now, in the present moment, and all that is in the present will lead you to your final destination.

Do not worry about the outcome, the destination. Spend your time . . . your precious, valuable time, concentrating on the moment. For it is the journey that is important, not the outcome, and if you miss the journey, if you are not present for the *gift of the now*, you will have missed the point and the destination will not matter.

Trust. Have faith and believe that as you take care of this moment, I am taking care of the next.

DAY 327: Are You Stuck in Your Comfort Zone?

Look at your beliefs. Look at your wants and your desires. Reach deep inside yourself and look for the blocks that are holding you back, the beliefs you have. Look at the steps you are taking to move away from where you are. See if you need to take different steps, make different choices. See if you need to take bigger risks, if you're taking any risks at all.

You can't step into your power zone if you're stuck in your comfort zone. Are you willing to be uncomfortable? Are you willing to let go of the familiar to own your power? I'd hazard a guess that if you're very, very comfortable where you are, you're not moving forward in big enough ways. Because when you're moving forward in really big ways, you're always going to be uncomfortable because you're always going to be unsure of where the path is taking you, where you're going to end up, and how it's all going to work out.

Some of you stay small because you are afraid, because you want to know and there's no way you *can* know, and so you hold yourself back instead of taking that leap of faith.

The bridge you need often doesn't appear until you step out into space. Are you willing to step out? Are you willing to take a risk? Are you ready to be more? It's up to you. Whatever you want, I support.

DAY 328: We're Here to Help

I'm not a quick fix. I know that's what some of you want Me to be.

Understand that I'm here to *support* you. I'm here to support your actions and your choices. I'm not here to do it *for* you; I'm here to *help you* do it, to help you recognize how strong you are, how many gifts and talents you have. That's what we're all here for, just waiting to be asked. How long will it take you to ask?

DAY 329: *Do Your Best*

Make choices that support the you that you *want* to be, not choices that support the you that you *used* to be.

I'm not saying you have to be perfect. I *am* saying do the best you can. Know that whatever choice you make, however many times you make it, I am always with you, supporting you as you make that choice. I am always with you, *always with you.*

DAY 330: *Ask Us for Something*

Perhaps you need to explore yourself more deeply, to know yourself better, to know what you want and what you don't want, what you're ready for and what you're willing to receive. Then tell Me . . . tell *all of us* who are here just waiting to assist you.

Once you tell us, we can begin the work. We may not give you what it is you said you wanted, but when you say what you think you need or what you want, it gives us permission to begin to work.

We then tune into *exactly* what it is you need and the perfect way to offer it to you.

So just say, "Yes!" Ask us for *something*, anything. Just start so we can start.

DAY 331: What's the True Path to Freedom?

You humans need to know. You need to be in control. Letting go of that control is so difficult for you! Surrender. That word scares so many of you; and yet, surrendering is the only true path to freedom.

What do you need to surrender? When will you *start*? That's all I'm asking . . . a baby step in the direction of surrendering. What baby step can you take? The sooner you start, the easier it will be.

DAY 332: Acknowledge All That You Are

Acknowledge your greatness! Acknowledge your power, your goodness, your specialness, your uniqueness, for you are—each and every one of you—a powerful, amazing being! How can you not be, made in the image and likeness of Me?

I create nothing short of perfection. Even that which you see as an imperfection, I see as perfection. The weaknesses, the imperfections, the things you consider negative about yourself, are all things you need in your life in order to learn and grow and be more; to experience the things your *souls* came here to experience.

All of you is perfect just the way it is; nothing less than perfect.

DAY 333: Put Both Feet on Each Step

Understand, *I am not going to show you the ultimate goal.* If I did that for you now, it would scare the pants off of you because you're not ready to do what I'm going to ask you to do when you get there. You don't have the tools. You don't have the experience. You don't have the belief in yourself or the trust in Me . . . *yet.*

I will show you one step at a time. I will light one step in front of you and ask you to put your foot upon it. When you are ready to rest *both* feet upon the same step, when both feet are on the same step and balanced, and you can pause there easily and effortlessly, you will know you are ready for the next step. And then *that step* will be lit for you.

You cannot walk safely and balanced if one foot is on the step ahead and one is on the step behind. It's not a good way to move forward. Show Me that you are committed to moving forward by putting one foot then the other on the *same* step, doing all you need to do to finish *that* step and *then I will light the next.*

And you will know, you will know deep within you, it is the right step and the right thing to do. *You will know.*

DAY 334: Know Me

Make Me be what you need Me to be to get close to Me. What name do you call Me? Do you call Me any name at all? Do you call Me God or Spirit or Allah? Do you say the Universe? The Great I Am?

I don't care if you call Me Ralph or Susie or Sam or Billy or Bob. Call Me whatever name will let you come closer to Me, not a name that makes you feel separate from Me because you think I am better, I am bigger, and you are not worthy.

I want you to know Me as friend, as lover, as parent, as child. I want you to know Me as the deepest part of yourself.

DAY 335: Love Yourself into Wholeness

You are *exactly* where you're supposed to be. You just need to relax into that. Allow yourself to recognize the appropriateness of where you are now and why you need to be where you are.

You have so many gifts to offer others who come into your life, but so many more gifts would be available to you if you could better heal the foundation of your own being. What is it that you're holding there, and why are you holding it? What purpose is it serving? Is it still a viable purpose or are there other ways you can heal, other ways you can take care of yourself, other ways you could do what you need to do to love yourself better?

That's what this journey is about: loving yourself better, loving yourself into wholeness.

DAY 336: Choose Your Vibration

You came to be of service, and each person that comes into your energy field has come for a reason. There are no accidents; there is no perhaps or maybe. That person has definitely come into your aura for a reason.

You don't need to know the reason. You just need to accept there is one. If you can accept that, you then must work to be your very best self so you are the highest vibration you can be to have the greatest impact. Because when you are at your highest vibration, you have the greatest impact in the best possible way. But keep in mind, if you vibrate at a low vibration, you also have an impact. That impact pulls others down instead of lifting them up.

You have a choice. You have a choice to be a high vibration or a lower vibration. Only you can determine your vibration.

DAY 337: Open Yourself to Deeper Healing

What is it you're *really* afraid of? You allow your fears to guide your actions, your thoughts, your emotions, your feelings, and you do that so you don't have to take a step forward. You are afraid of where stepping out and stepping up may lead you.

Although you may not like where you are, it *is* familiar. You know how to be who you are where you are. But if you were to step out, step out of your box and open yourself to new experiences, to more risk, to expansion and transformation, you don't have an image in your mind of what that would look like or feel like. You have no idea what might be expected of you.

So, for some of you, perhaps even many of you, you keep yourself playing small so you don't have to put yourself into an unfamiliar environment where, if you are honest with yourself, you are afraid you might fail.

But if you can open yourself to a deeper healing—if you can allow that which you've been holding onto for so long, consciously and unconsciously, to rise to the surface, allow Me to take it from you, and then take the steps you need to take to step out of the box you've put yourself in—there will be miracles. There will be amazing experiences. There will be higher highs than you can even imagine!

Sure, there will be lows; there will be darker times and difficult times. There will be challenging times. For as high as you might go, you will then also have to go as deep. There cannot be one without the other, two sides of the same coin, opposites.

Both necessary for your healing, your growth and learning, your expansion. And it's nothing, nothing at all that you haven't asked for in stating what it was you wanted to learn in this human existence.

DAY 338: Be More

Be more of who you came here to be. Open your heart in bigger ways, in new ways, in new ways that *challenge* you to grow and be more. You have a long journey yet ahead of you, and much you can do to impact the welfare of others, the well being of others.

Ask yourself how else you can serve. Pay attention to the opportunities that come to you. Discern which opportunities that present themselves will make you happy in serving and which ones will drain you. Choose those that will add to your life, not diminish it. Choose those that will allow you to add to the lives of others. There is so much more you can offer.

DAY 339: Put Your Human Responsibilities First

Remember, you are human and spirit combined. As spirit, you chose to become human to learn that which you could only learn in your human form. Because of that, it is your *human responsibilities* that *must come first!* It is through those that you are learning what you need to learn.

Some of you will feel that the human responsibilities are holding you back and are an impediment because your soul longs to soar. It is important to understand that in taking care of those you came here to take care of, you are enabling your spirit to learn and grow and heal itself, to expand in new ways because of the choices you have made about that which you wish to learn in this incarnation.

DAY 340: Give Me a Moment Tonight

Tonight, just before you go to sleep, take a moment—a concentrated, intentional moment—and let Me know if you're willing to connect with Me. Just let Me know. And if you tell Me yes and you continue to take steps to show Me your continued willingness, you'll begin to see shifts and changes take place in your life. Your path will open. Your footsteps will quicken. Your impact will be greater and you will be doing exactly what you came here to do.

That's all I need: a moment of your time tonight, *an intentional moment*, a brief conversation and connection. I don't even care if you're lying in your bed in your jammies when it happens, as long as you take the time, make a space, and talk to Me.

I'll be waiting. I hope you show up.

DAY 341: *Your Angels' Request*

The journeys are never easy, even when they seem so, even when it seems like you know exactly where you are going and for what purpose. The journey itself is what you are being called to be present to—not the end result, not the anticipated reward, only the journey. For it is on the journey, walking the path, that the greatest gifts come.

If you are aware and alert and open, the messages and gifts seem greater and more frequent because you *are* aware. You are being guided and we have your best interest at heart in a way that is different from those who are less aware and less trusting. It does not mean we are not equally present for them; it only means they are less present to our presence.

Better that you see a message in every occurrence than ignore them because you think the guidance would not come in such a way. We speak to you in the way we think we can reach you most and best, but sometimes in our haste to speak to you, we forget that you are waiting for the big booming voice, rather than the subtle whisper in your ear.

We ask again, repeating ourselves, that you be more present and more open to *all* that is around you, within and without, for the guidance will take different forms and come at different times. Err on the side of seeing too much, rather than missing or ignoring, for all will come to you as it is meant to if you are patient and willing to receive.

DAY 342: Think Vibration

Think *vibration*—not right or wrong—think *vibration*. Get rid of judgment and criticism. When you judge and criticize yourself, it is much more difficult to get unstuck because it feels like no matter what you do, you can't do the right thing or do enough. So simply think *higher vibration choice* and make the best choice you can each time you have the opportunity to make a choice, no matter how small.

Recognize when you have chosen the lesser vibration, the lower vibration. Ask yourself, "Why? What motivated that choice rather than the higher choice?" Don't judge yourself for the reason why, but in looking at those choices help yourself understand what is going on within you, where you need to put some extra attention, where you need to give yourself some extra love, where you need to be perhaps more charitable with yourself, more compassionate. When you do this, you will notice that more and more often you choose the higher vibration choice because it is what calls to you. It is where you yearn to be.

I will be honest and tell you that it will not be an easy task. More often than not, you will want to go for the lower vibration because it will take less of your time and your energy. It will be the *easier* choice. But you will see time and again as you choose the lower vibration that your own vibration is lowered and you will not feel as good—mentally, physically, emotionally or spiritually. You will notice that every single time you choose the higher vibration, *you feel better*—mentally, physically, emotionally and spiritually.

Soon you will *yearn* for that higher vibration to go through you completely, on every level, every moment of every day. So, more and more you will choose the higher choice. Be aware. Be aware of what you feel in your body, in your heart. Be aware of the thoughts you think. Be aware of the feelings you feel each and every time you make a choice. Take note. And allow that to help you understand what it is you need to help yourself heal, so that more and more often you have the courage and the energy to choose the higher choice.

Know that no matter what choice you make, I am always with you. I am always supporting you. I am always doing all I can to assist you with the choices you *have* made.

DAY 343: Spread Your Wings and Fly

Take flight. Allow yourself to leave the safety of the nest and spread your wings and fly. Do not worry about your final destination. Allow the current of Spirit to lift your wings and guide and direct you. It is all you really need if you trust in Spirit.

Like the baby birds whose mothers often push them from the nest's edge, we would often like to give you that same gentle, loving nudge. But you have been given the gift of free will—freedom of choice—so unlike the mother bird, we must sit silently by and wait until *you* make the choice to leave the nest. We cannot interfere with your freedom to choose.

This gift is a gift given without attachment, to be used by the receiver as the receiver chooses, not as the Giver would have the gift used; so this Divine gift is yours to use as you choose, without worry about recriminations or punishment, without guilt. Know that it is the ultimate gift given by the ultimate Giver, and however you choose to use it, it will be used as it was meant to be used.

Are we always patient as we wait beside you, waiting to see when, or even if, you will choose to leave the nest? No, but we wait with love and understanding of the difficulties you feel are in front of you as you contemplate taking that first step, having not yet experienced that current of faith beneath your wings that is ready to support you and take you higher.

Or perhaps you have experienced that wind beneath your wings before, but in smaller matters, and so this time, with a greater leap being contemplated, you are still unsure if that smaller wind that supported you before will be strong enough to support you now.

Have no fear—or leap in spite of your fear—for whatever you need to walk in faith is always given you, no matter how great the distance you choose to leap. There is no shortage, no weakness, no lack; there is only *all that you need*, if only you have the faith to take the first step and leave the comfort of the nest.

We are waiting. We are by your side. We are here. Trust us, trust in this. Spread your wings and fly.

DAY 344: You Are All Co-Creators

Remember this as you go through your journey: As the experiences come and go, remember *you chose* what it is you are experiencing. We are here to help in any way we can and we will, when you ask us to. If you choose not to ask for help, we do not give help because we do not intrude. But if you ask, help is given. Release your expectation as to the form the help will take. Trust that how it comes is the best way for what you need to learn, for what your *soul* sought to learn, in this lifetime.

Do not blame your parents, or your spouse, or the children. Do not blame your teachers. Do not blame those you felt could have loved you better and didn't. *You* are making the choices, and you have asked all of those who came into this present incarnation with you to do what they have done, to help you learn what you came here to learn.

You are all co-creators. No one is at fault. *All* are responsible, but *there is no one to blame.* All of you are accountable for the journeys, the lessons, the experiences that are coming to you. Remember this the next time you get angry with someone, the next time you wish to point a finger or blame someone. Remember that *you are co-creating the experience* because each of you needs to learn something from it.

The lessons, of course, will be different. You need yours, they need theirs. But *all* lessons will be learned from *that* experience, and each lesson will be different because the perspective of each one learning will be different from the other. You will get exactly what you need each and every time, whether you realize it or not, whether you like it or not. It will be *exactly* what you need it to be.

DAY 345: *How to Get from A to B*

Release your expectations. Detach from the outcome of your choices. Quit labeling yourself and your choices and just see them for what they are: this is what it is at this moment in time.

Now, how do I proceed from here? What is the best course of action to take? How do I get from point A, where I am, to point B, where I'd like to be? And what seems to be the best way to make that journey, that transition?

Whatever your answer is, move on that without an expectation of how it will come out. When you get to where you're going, stop and make the next decision. Review where you've been and how it worked and from that point of view, make the next choice. It really *is* that simple.

DAY 346: Move Forward with Detachment

It is always best to come to us with detachment. Have an intention, but move forward with detachment, trusting that the outcome will always be determined by Spirit when you come seeking Spirit's assistance and guidance and help.

Set your intention. Do your work. Show Me that you come intentionally, *prepared* to do your work. That is why you set your own intention. But then detach from that intention. Detach from the outcome of your intention, and know and have faith that what you receive will be exactly what we know you need.

Those of us in spirit know you far better than you know yourself. Your judgments can be clouded by the tension and stress of your day, by the needs of others, by your exhaustion. So come with detachment. Come intending to be fully present. Come intending to receive whatever is being offered and given, knowing that it will be perfect from the point of the Divine and your Divine path and purpose in this lifetime.

DAY 347: Sit Within the Is-Ness

You humans! You want it to be done here and now! You think that if it doesn't happen here and now in *your* time, it's not going to happen at all.

You have to get away from criticism, self-criticism and self-judgment. You have to just see things as "this is what it is" without a label. Good, bad or otherwise, just let it be what it is. Just sit within that is-ness and let it work, let it be.

DAY 348: Recognize Your Greatness

Recognize the greatness that is within you! *Honor* that greatness! *Express* that greatness! But express it with humility and humbleness, recognizing that *all you are* is a gift from Me, that *each* of you is simply a channel for all that I am because *you and I are One.*

When you reach your hands out to assist another, I am reaching out *through your hands*. So I need you. *I need you!*

I'm asking you to continue to grow and expand. Find new ways to express yourself and use your gifts. Find new ways to explore and uncover those gifts that are still within you and not yet known, because there are many!

It will be an exciting journey, I promise you. There will be bumps along the way. There will be sadness as well as happiness, but that is what life is all about. In the end, though, you will look back and know that you have been truly blessed, truly blessed!

DAY 349: Your Journey Has a Purpose

Lightness and darkness, pain and pleasure, black and white, wrong and right: all come from the same source, the Divine Source of All That Is. There is a purpose to your journey, a purpose to your pain, your discomfort and your dis-ease, just as there is purpose in your pleasure and your bliss and your rapture.

So often when you are caught up in one or the other, you forget to ask what it is you are learning, what this has come to teach you. When you are caught up in your pain, it is much easier to say, "Why me?" When you are happy and blissful, and things are going well, it is so easy to forget to say "Thank you," to be present to all you have.

But *all* comes from the same source, with the same purpose: to teach you, to bring you from where you are to where you should be going, to where you *desire* to go. The method of transition is your *choice*, a choice you made long ago. And now that you are in the midst of all you have requested so you can learn the lessons you need to learn, you have forgotten you have made the request. It makes the journey much more difficult because you do not know, because you are questioning.

But if you knew, there would be no lesson in the learning. It is in the *experience* that the teaching occurs, the learning happens, the growing and the expansion. You need the experiences, the pleasure as well as the pain, the bliss as well as the sorrow . . . two sides of the same coin, two ends of the same spectrum. All come to teach you that which you have *requested* to learn.

Can you detach from what you are feeling? Can you step back and recognize a bigger hand in this? A bigger picture? If you can, the journey gets easier. You are not so caught up in the questions: "Why me?" . . . "What did I do to deserve this?"

So much to learn, so little time! Your journey here, in reality, is short, just a blink of the eye in the Divine space of time. You have all the time you need though, to do all that it is you came here to do. You just need to *recognize* that you do and trust in it. When you are feeling pressured and under the gun, so to speak, step back and take a breath . . . and breathe! Put yourself in a place of peacefulness and calm.

DAY 350: Talk to Me

I am only asking you to do what I am giving you guidance and direction and support and tools to do. Listen to your heart as you go forward. Err on the side of less rather than more.

So if a message comes to you and you are not exactly sure what to do with it, if it seems too big, if it seems like it would cause a huge problem, you're not sure whether it's Divine or ego, then talk to Me and ask for additional information. Ask, "What do I do with this? Why are you giving this to me?"

Understand that you are in control of what you receive and what you do not. If there's information you truly do not want to know, if it begins to come through and it frightens you, or it seems more than you are willing to handle, I have no problem with you saying to Me, "This is further than I wish to go. This is not what I wish to receive." I won't punish you. I won't think badly of you. I will hear you are making a choice and I will honor that choice and support it.

If things are happening too quickly, if you need Me to slow down, tell Me that. But *tell* Me, don't just drag your feet . . . *tell* Me! Have an open, honest conversation with Me from your heart space and let Me know what is happening. Let Me know your fears and your worries. Because only when you talk to Me, only when you choose to share with Me, can I be of help. I cannot intrude, nor can any of the guides and messengers who are working with you. You have freedom of choice, and I honor that regardless of the choices you make. Every choice you make—hear Me, *every choice you make*— is supported by Me.

If you want My help, if you want My assistance, if there is something that needs to be altered for you to be able to do My work in a better way, that fits better for who you are and where you are in this stage of your journey, talk to Me. Tell Me. Be open and honest. For unlike your parents or other figures in authority, *I will hear you*. I will not criticize you. I will not tell you that you should not feel what you feel or want what you want.

I will be where you are. I will always encourage you to be more. That is My job. My desire for each and every one of you is that you'll reach the pinnacle of all you are capable of.

DAY 351: *Own Your Truth*

It is easy to make excuses, to find reasons to put things off, to find reasons to say no instead of yes or yes instead of no. It is easy to *rationalize* that the choices you are making are the *real* choices, the *best* choices, and you can find all the reasons in the world and *more,* to validate that for yourself.

But there is this niggling little piece of you, down deep inside, that knows you are rationalizing and denying and making excuses because you are afraid, because you are not yet ready, because you want things to be a certain way before you say yes or before you say no. Until they are that certain way, you feel you are justified in holding back an action that you know will take you the farthest.

You have to let go of your ego and your pride. You have to bend down low in supplication. You have to surrender. You have to give it up. And then you have to decide *not to take it back*, once you've given it up.

DAY 352: Be Intentional and Focused

When the world becomes too much for you, when the chaos is dragging you down, that's when it's most important for you to sit in the silence and reconnect with Me. No talking is needed. No words need to be said, no promises made. Just sit and be present; allow us to connect.

When you sit in the silence you allow Me to know that you want My presence, that you want the connection, that you are making a time and space for that to happen.

You are all so good at multi-tasking. You want to pray when you're driving on the highway or when you're doing the dishes or when you're working or walking. But I'm asking you to be intentional and focused when you want to connect with Me. Just simply sit in the silence and be.

DAY 353: *Change Keeps You Going*

Do not be afraid to open up to change. Allow that which is occurring in front of you and around you to continue in its own time, in its own way, at its own pace. Do not force your ways upon others just because they work for *you*. Remember that to be the messenger of change, you, yourself must be open to change, for if you are not, how can you expect others to change?

You are no different from those around you. Remember this as you go forward. You are no better or no worse. You are equal yet different. To see yourself as better than others will cause you to stumble on the path and will make it more difficult to move forward. Being stuck in your ways, however well they have worked for you in the past, will keep you stuck in the present, incapable of and unready for the move into tomorrow.

Change, always change. Allow it, welcome it, embrace it. It is what keeps you going. It is what's necessary for life. Change, change, change.

DAY 354: *Give and Receive*

I know for some of you it's very difficult to ask for help, but I want you to start thinking of asking for help as a gift you offer to those you ask. What a blessing it is to be able to give to someone in need! What a blessing to be able to receive and not always be the giver! When you are strong enough to ask for help, then accept help from someone else, they will be more likely to be willing to ask for help when *they* need it. How wonderful if all of you could begin to do that for one another!

So many gifts, so much power, so much wisdom and information, so much experience, so much to share, to give, to receive! Use the connections. Don't do it alone if you don't have to. It's all well and good to ask Me for help. I'm always here; your guides and angels, likewise.

But sometimes you really need help here on the earth plane in the form of physical helpers, so it's really important you learn to ask and that you receive gratefully and gracefully. It's important that when someone offers help, even if it's not offered in the exact way you would like it to be, you say yes anyway, because just because it's not the way you want it to be doesn't mean it won't help.

There's value in receiving. There's value in giving. There's a balance in the universe, so you need to both give and receive.

DAY 355: Hold Your Hands in Prayer

Quit assigning blame. You need to quit putting labels on things: good or bad, black or white, right or wrong. You just need to see what is, as what is. Accept it and move on. Quit calling yourself "victim" or others "perpetrators." Quit pointing your finger at others and saying, "It's their fault!"

Instead, hold your hands together in prayer and look within. Take responsibility and be accountable for your own choices and your own actions. It will take you so much farther than pointing the finger outward.

DAY 356: *Empower Your Dreams*

It is your own journey. You have set the path. You've chosen what you've come here to learn. Granted, at the time you chose, you were in spirit. So sometimes when you are in spirit and make those choices, you think you are more capable.

You don't understand the difficulties of being human, not because you haven't been human before, because you have. But when you're in spirit, the energy of spirit takes precedence, and you think you are as powerful when you are in human form as you are when you are spirit. Then you come into your humanness and find that you are limited *because you are human* and do not have the powers you have when you are in spirit. You find that the choices, the decisions you made in spirit, are much more difficult to enact when you are in your physical body. They take a lot more work, a lot more effort, a lot more determination and faith and trust.

It's okay if you don't fulfill *all of them* this time around. You can do it again next time. Again, there is no judgment—not from Me, not from any of your teachers or guides or mentors. We just sit and watch and help when we can, when you allow us to. We facilitate your forward movement, and we facilitate your standing still. You'll understand this all so much better when you leave this physical body, when you can sit once again in spirit and look back at it all and see the path that opened up before you because of the choices you made. It will make so much more sense then.

But you're in human form now, so you have lots of questions about the whys and the wherefores and the hows and the whens. Sometimes there is resentment, anger, guilt, fear and doubt, and they get in the way.

It's up to you to be strong enough to make the choices to empower your dreams, to have the faith and trust you need to take that leap of faith. We are all here for you, always. We will facilitate the perfect outcome in whatever way we can when you take the steps you need to take to help yourself move forward.

DAY 357: *Be an Instrument of Peace*

Pray for peace, send peace and be peace to all you love, to all who love you, to all you've wronged, to all who have wronged you. Send out peace and healing to strangers you pass on the street, to strangers you see from afar and to those who are too far to see.

Reach out in love to all. Choose to be an instrument *of* peace, *for* peace, *with* peace. Make a conscious choice in your life to be better, different, more than you have ever been before until this point in time.

Do not see yourself as small or inconsequential. See yourself as a powerful instrument of all that is good and right and holy; all that is Divine, all that comes from that one Source that unites all, connects all, touches all. Be the messenger, the channel, the instrument of peace and healing, and see the changes in all those around you.

Be patient and forgiving. Be accepting. Allow all to be where they are, where they are meant to be, as you are who you are and where you are meant to be. Simply practice being and giving in this new way, from this new place of being an instrument, and watch and wait and see. Miracles will happen. Some small, some large, some minuscule, some mighty. But miracles *will* occur. Trust and see. Believe.

DAY 358: *Untether Yourself*

You cannot soar to new heights if you are still tethered to the earth. No matter how long a cord you have given yourself, as long as you are still tethered, there is only so far you can go.

DAY 359: You Only Have One Purpose

What is your purpose? Why are you here? What did you come to do? So many of you ask those questions over and over and over. You're so busy asking, and then so busy telling yourself why you can't possibly do what it is you think you've heard you should be doing, that you don't allow yourself to take in the answer. You don't allow yourself to have the knowingness.

I'm going to give you a hint today—actually, much more than a hint. I'm going to tell you that your purpose, *your only purpose*, is to be your best self. That's all you came here to do, *be your best self.*

DAY 360: Do Your Inner Work

Who do you *want* to be? Who do you think you are now? What is it that you think is lacking or still needs to be addressed? Where do you need to put your *energy,* your *focus,* your *intention,* to assist you in an even better way as you walk this path?

The only one who has the answers to these questions is you. If you are not spending the time you need to go inward and focus on self, the answers will not come to you. Moving forward takes action, both internally and externally. You must clear the path within you in order to clear the path in front of you. They are two paths, but they are not separate paths. They are two parts of the whole, and until both of them are addressed, you will stay where you are.

So remember to do the *inner* work as well as take the outer action. Combining the two will move you forward in amazing ways, ways you cannot even begin to imagine. But the inner work is a must, and as you go higher, you *will* need to dig deeper.

DAY 361: Everything Affects Everything

So often you are caught up in feelings of lack, especially financial, and do not understand that when you feel there is a lack financially, you are also then bringing to you a lack in every other area of your life.

An opening in one area opens them all. A closing in one area tamps them all down. You are connected to all things in all ways, and if all things are connected, what you experience in one experience affects *all* your experiences.

DAY 362: Push Through Your Fear

There are those who say, "Have no fear." But what I will say to you is, having no fear is unrealistic. It is better to think about pushing *through your fear*, acknowledging you are fearful, but also deciding you will move forward *in spite of the fear*.

As you take action, your fear will begin to diminish because you will see, act by act, step by step, that you are successful. That is not to say it might not rear up its ugly head again and be there big and bold and powerful in front of you. But because you have already seen you can diminish it by taking your action steps, begin to take action again and see it diminish again. It's the ups and downs of the journey, the highs and the lows, and it's all about the journey and *how you handle* the highs and the lows.

DAY 363: I'm Ready to Help

Who are you? Who would you like to be? What are you dreaming of?

I know the longing of your heart. I know your deepest desires and your greatest dreams. I am here and ready to help when you are ready to say yes and surrender.

DAY 364: Relinquish and Surrender

You get too caught up in the negative and are too quick to judge yourself, more severe with yourself than with those you love and care about. Be gentle with yourself. Love yourself greatly.

Take action to show how much you love yourself by honoring your needs, by honoring your heart, by honoring the guidance you are receiving about what you should do in your life. Your guides and angels and I, we are always here for you. Ask us in, invite us to help.

And once you have asked us in and invited us, do not take back that invitation. Do not act out of fear and pull back, but instead, relinquish and surrender so that we can indeed take the reins and guide the next steps on your journey.

DAY 365: You Have a Special Purpose in this World

You are shining lights, each in your own way. You each have your own unique gifts and talents. So it stands to reason that how you are being called to serve is different for each of you, and may change over time as what we need from you changes, as those around you change, as the population you are here to serve changes.

Do not be stuck in old ways of being. Do not think there is only one thing, and one thing only, you are here to do. Do not think less of yourself or limit yourself, but open yourself to the possibility that all you can do is not yet known to you.

I am not saying don't set your sights. I am saying, don't narrow your vision. Keep your eyes wide open. Know that the possibilities are endless and that you really have no idea of the breadth and scope of the work you've been brought here to do. Nor do you know how many people you touch just by being who you are, vibrating at the vibration you vibrate at . . . a unique vibration unlike that of any other.

You have a special purpose in this world, and no one else can take your place. Understand that. *There is no one who can take your place!*

Straight Talk for Specific Needs

Good Advice

Day: 34, 44, 60, 73, 97, 134, 141, 307

Gratitude

Day: 80, 94, 164, 205, 299

Guidance about Guidance

Day: 67, 74, 100, 151, 184, 194, 208, 311, 316, 341, 350

Heal Yourself

Day: 45, 93, 131, 145, 160, 172, 203, 228, 249, 264, 314, 324, 337

Helping Others

Day: 93, 220, 295, 319, 336, 338, 365

Judgement and Criticism (of others)

Day: 13, 129, 291, 300, 305, 321

Judgement and Criticism (of self)

Day: 32, 43, 116, 209, 231, 257, 291, 297, 342

Labels

Day: 43, 60, 85, 97, 106, 153, 165, 355

Lack

Day: 65, 148, 361

Letting Go

Day: 2, 10, 12, 53, 63, 105, 135, 176, 230, 293, 303

Listen to Your Heart

Day: 15, 18, 38, 147, 163, 220, 256

Look Within

Day: 12, 67, 114, 187, 201, 274, 300, 303, 342, 355, 360

Self-acceptance
Day: 65, 102, 173, 209, 257, 310, 332
Self-care
Day: 15, 16, 29, 36, 103, 125, 133, 256, 264, 319
Stuck
Day: 22, 67, 68, 78, 113, 114, 135, 138, 230, 241, 327
Support
Day: 17, 78, 91, 111, 158, 223, 247, 285, 304, 309, 328
Surrender
Day: 3, 12, 20, 23, 167, 239, 244, 265, 331, 351, 363
Take Action
Day: 2, 24, 58, 68, 139, 191, 199, 206, 219, 254, 333, 362
The Journey
Day: 40, 53, 60, 86, 95, 101, 122, 161, 284, 318, 356
The Past
Day: 45, 88, 105, 135, 280, 262
Trust and Faith
Day: 84, 90, 127, 136, 174, 183, 193, 196, 225, 252, 343
Unanswered Prayers
Day: 9, 213, 248, 330
Victim Thinking
Day: 59, 85, 87, 122, 124, 132, 218, 266, 288, 344, 355
Words Have Energy
Day: 5, 13, 129

Why?

Day: 3, 30, 51, 60, 61, 288, 349

You Are Loved

Day: 27, 72, 83, 118, 142, 156, 211, 234, 283, 298

Your Gifts

Day: 31, 69, 121, 143, 162, 188, 196, 290, 335, 348, 365

Your Life's Plan

Day: 1, 87, 120, 132, 161, 197, 255, 258, 261, 284, 339, 356

Your Purpose

Day: 66, 119, 124, 179, 207, 295, 326, 336, 349, 359, 365

Walls

Day: 280, 281, 361

Additional Resources for Your Journey

I've been an avid reader for as long as I can remember. Books are strewn around my home, my office bookcases are filled to overflowing, and it's rare when I get into my car without a book on the passenger seat to keep me company on my travels.

My life experiences have taught me that God most often provides the guidance, direction and wisdom that we need in ways that are both familiar and comfortable. So I'm not surprised that the perfect books have come across my path exactly when I needed them in one way or another.

Because books have played such an important role in *my* life, I wanted to offer a selection of titles from my own library as additional resources for *your* journey. I hope you find them to be as helpful and enlightening as I have. Enjoy!

After the Ecstasy, the Laundry: How the Heart Grows Wise on the Spiritual Path by Jack Kornfield, PhD [Bantam Books, 2001]

Anatomy of the Spirit: The Seven Stages of Power and Healing by Caroline Myss, PhD [Crown Publishers, 1996]

Angel Numbers: The Angels Explain the Meaning of 111, 444, and Other Numbers in Your Life by Doreen Virtue, PhD and Lynnette Brown [Hay House, 2005]

Animal Speak: The Spiritual & Magical Powers of Creatures Great & Small by Ted Andrews [Llewellyn Publications, 2003]

Animal Spirit Guides: An Easy-to-Use Handbook for Identifying and Understanding Your Power Animals and Animal Spirit Helpers by Steven Farmer, PhD [Hay House, 2006]

Archangels & Ascended Masters: A Guide to Working and Healing with Divinities and Deities by Doreen Virtue, PhD [Hay House, 2003]

Ask and It Is Given: Learning to Manifest Your Desires by Esther and Jerry Hicks [Hay House, 2004]

A Woman's Journey to God: Finding the Feminine Path by Joan Borysenko, PhD [Riverhead Books, 1999]

Born Knowing: A Medium's Journey, Accepting and Embracing My Spiritual Gifts by John Holland [Hay House, 2003]

Callings: Finding and Following an Authentic Life by Gregg Levoy [Three Rivers Press, 1997]

Conversations with God: An Uncommon Dialogue, book 1 by Neale Donald Walsch [G.P. Putnam's Sons, 1995]

Divine Guidance: How to Have a Dialogue with God and Your Guardian Angels by Doreen Virtue, PhD [Renaissance Books, 1998]

God Calling: A Devotional Diary by A. J. Russell [Barnes and Noble Books, 2002]

Heal Your Body: The Mental Causes for Physical Illness and the Metaphysical Way to Overcome Them by Louise L. Hay [Hay House, 1988]

Invisible Acts of Power: Personal Choices That Create Miracles by Caroline Myss, PhD [Free Press, 2004]

Journey of Souls: Case Studies of Life Between Lives by Michael Newton, PhD [Llewellyn Publications, 2004]

Many Lives, Many Masters: Messages from the Masters by Brian Weiss, MD [One Spirit, 2002]

The Eagle and The Rose: A Remarkable True Story by Rosemary Altea [Warner Vision Books, 1995]

The Law of Attraction: The Basics of the Teachings of Abraham by Esther and Jerry Hicks [Hay House, 2006]

When God Winks at You: How God Speaks Directly to You Through the Power of Coincidence by Squire Rushnell [MJF Books, 2006]

Why People Don't Heal and How They Can by Caroline Myss, PhD [Three Rivers Press, 1997]

You Can Heal Your Life by Louise L. Hay [Hay House, 1987]

You Own the Power: Stories and Exercises to Inspire and Unleash the Force Within by Rosemary Altea [Quill, 2001]

About the Author

Bonnie Hassan, MSW, has had a private practice as a Reiki Master, medium, channel, psychic and psychotherapist since 2003.

In 1991, Bonnie had a direct encounter with God after uttering a prayer in church. Unable to finish the thesis that was required for her undergraduate degree, Bonnie surrendered it to Spirit as she knelt in prayer. A warm rush of blue energy washed over her from above and she began to cry. Upon returning home, the only thing Bonnie remembers is changing her clothes and sitting at the computer. Eight hours later, she "came to" just as her 100-page thesis spilled from the printer. That answered prayer was Bonnie's introduction to an intimate relationship with the Divine that continues to this day.

Since that time, Bonnie has completed her bachelor of science degree in human resource management and master's degree in social work. She became a Reiki Master in Usui/Tibetan Reiki in 2000 and followed that with master certifications in Karuna™ Reiki and Sekhem-Seichim-Reiki.

In 2003, Bonnie saw a vision of Mary, the Blessed Mother, during her spiritual practice. In it, Mary told her, "I have work for you to do and you can't do it here." Following the guidance she received, Bonnie left her job as a therapist and opened a private healing practice in Pittsburgh, Pennsylvania. She combined her expertise as a therapist with her training as a Reiki Master to offer unique individual healing sessions while also teaching classes in Usui/Tibetan and Karuna™ Reiki.

As Bonnie's practice grew, her spiritual and intuitive gifts began to unfold. Bonnie was guided to offer group healing sessions in which she began spontaneously channeling messages from God. She also began teaching Transformational Reiki (a new form of Reiki combining Japanese and Native American energies) that evolved as her gifts developed.

Bonnie relocated to Nashville, Tennessee in 2013 to be a hands-on grandmother to her new granddaughter, Hayden. Once there, she opened a new practice. In addition to her in-person work in Nashville, Bonnie offers a weekly healing session via teleconference to people around the world and travels extensively in the United States sharing her unique gifts with both groups and individuals. She continues to offer training in Transformational Reiki and all levels of Usui/Tibetan and Karuna™ Reiki.

Through both her private and group healing sessions and Reiki classes, Bonnie has helped thousands of individuals develop their own intimate connection with God and find the clarity and healing necessary for their individual life journeys.

Bonnie can be reached at bonnie@bonniehassan.com or www.bonniehassan.com.